Foundations of Living

By the same author
Echoes of Life

Foundations of Living

Insights for an Enriching Life

DR AJAYPAL KALYAN

BOLD

An imprint of
Srishti Publishers & Distributors

Srishti Publishers & Distributors
A unit of AJR Publishing LLP
212A, Peacock Lane
Shahpur Jat, New Delhi – 110 049

editorial@srishtipublishers.com

First published by Bold,
an imprint of Srishti Publishers & Distributors in 2024

10 9 8 7 6 5 4 3 2 1

Printed and bound in India.

For my Parents

&

Readers who want to transform their lives...

Truth does not make a man great. It is man's actions that make the truth great.

—Confucius

Contents

Acknowledgments

It has been a deeply insightful experience for me to write this book, and I am thankful for all those who've stood behind me as I poured my thoughts into this book.

To my family, thank you for always supporting me when I needed you the most.

Writing has always been a very lonely endeavour but when you have friends behind you, you can never feel the lonesomeness.

So, to all my friends and colleagues, thank you for your valuable feedback and insights, and most importantly, your time.

I also owe a great deal to the many other thinkers and writers whose works have accompanied me through this voyage, helping to light my path to writing better.

To the readers, whose enquiring minds and willingness to hear new points of view make this endeavour worthwhile. The final indicator of this book's impact will be your engagement with these ideas.

Finally, I wish to express my deepest gratitude to all those who believe in the transformative power of knowledge and self-discovery. This book is as much yours as it is mine. Thank you.

Preface

There is an age-old adage: Man is born free but spends the rest of his life in chains. Remarkably, this saying resonates even in today's frenetic world. At birth, children enter the world untethered, unrestrained by convention. Yet, as they grow and begin to crawl, walk, and talk, society imposes a set of rules upon them.

"Eat with your right hand," they are told.

"Think logically,"

"Don't do this,"

"Don't go there," and the list goes on.

When a child embarks on their educational journey, they are subtly directed toward a specific line of thinking.

"You excel in logical thinking? Consider a career in science."

"You possess a penchant for thinking outside the box? The arts await your exploration."

"Proficient in mathematics? Become an accountant, and the path is laid."

The next phase of life is spent as a devoted partner and a nurturing parent. While it may not be fair to label it as imprisonment, one's freedom is undoubtedly constrained during this period. Dreams and ambitions take a backseat as the responsibility of providing for the family takes centre stage. Finally, in the twilight years, individuals are often bound by the chains of various bodily ailments until their journey comes to an end.

Yet, throughout their lifetime, individuals frequently perceive themselves as superior to their peers. While this self-assurance can drive ambition, it is not always for the good. This self-assurance can also lead to avarice and complacency. Which begs the question, why do people undergo this transformation, despite being confined to a particular mindset? This has confounded philosophers for generations, and the answer remains elusive. Nevertheless, glimpses of insight have emerged throughout human history.

One approach to this question is to trace humanity's journey from the dawn of civilization and all the way to one's personal development. Jean-Jacques Rousseau, in his treatise *The Social Contract*, proposes a unique perspective. He posits that as long as a group of people is obligated to follow directives, they would do so because individuals within a group tend to imitate the actions of others in order to fit in. However, when one individual manages to break free from this yoke of conformity, they often end up outperforming their peers. Rousseau argues that when personal freedom is unjustly curtailed without providing any solid reason, individuals would be justified in reclaiming it. Yet, he also contends that in a just society, there exists a solid foundation for humans to act and comply as a collective. He states that the norms for the actions of the collective are based on established conventions rather than just a whim.

This begs the question: Do these conventions and norms truly serve their purpose? Why establish them if we cannot predict how individuals will react? Who was accorded the power to establish these norms and made them custodians? And who would watch over the custodians themselves? To answer these questions, we must embark on a reflective journey from the dawn of society and all the way to the development of an individual itself.

With this in mind, this book explores various ideas put forth by past philosophers. It is intentionally written in a manner that seeks to be objective by focusing on various facets of the journey and refrains from seeking validation for specific points. Furthermore, it eschews a direct dialogue with the audience, and instead opts for a more straightforward approach to convey the revelations born from this journey.

Today's audience lives in societies that grapple with a constant shortage of personal time. Keeping this concern at the back of the pocket, this book is penned in a colloquial style to connect with the reader, taking them on a spiritual journey of self-realization to enhance their lives. The ideas presented in this book elucidate the thoughts of different philosophers in a manner accessible to the everyday person, assuming limited familiarity with philosophical history.

Critics may argue that these profound philosophical ideas have been diluted, but true philosophy was always intended to be in a form that everybody would understand and incorporate in their lives. This book's core purpose is to make everyone comprehend the origins of civilized society, the evolution of life to its current state, and how to harness our existence for self-realization. It's important to acknowledge that pinpointing the exact influences of philosophies in shaping our society is nearly impossible. We can only speculate on its developmental processes, and thus the modern approach taken to writing this book.

Without further ado, this book draws inspiration from the works of four great philosophers of their time: Jean-Jacques Rousseau's *The Social Contract*, Friedrich Nietzsche's *Beyond Good and Evil*, Henry David Thoreau's *Walden*, and Lin Yutang's *The Importance of Living*. Each treatise contributes distinct insights into the journey that shall be undertaken in this book.

Our odyssey begins with the genesis of societies and progresses to the acquisition of civil rights by the strongest. We shall then explore the significance of a social contract within a civilized society and how it can be influenced by sovereign entities, including dictators, censorship, and various aspects of government. This is followed by an examination of the economic landscape and its impact on individual freedom, as well as its role in shaping philosophical perspectives. We would then consequently use this as a foundation to delve into the evolution of morality in humans, the concept of virtue, and the defining traits of nobility. Ultimately, we shall embark on the path to self-realization by exploring what it means to be human, how to find joy in life, dissecting the drawbacks of materialism, and discovering happiness through travel, living, and spirituality. The journey culminates with the art of thinking as a means of attaining self-realization.

***

Chapter 1

The Origins of Society

Society originates because an individual alone is not self-sufficient and no two of us are born alike.

—Aristotle

Imagine this scenario: In the distant past, mankind has just evolved past its primitive ape origins and had begun actively hunting for food rather than scrounging for it. In a pivotal moment, the earliest human ancestors uncovered fire. Though in hindsight it was more a discovery and not an invention, it united our primitive ancestors and began fostering communal living by the newfound source of warmth. Around this fire, the minds of the collective group converged and realized that the new found heat tenderized the hunted meat, making it more palatable. As time passed, the collective minds were put to work again and discerned that certain plants enhanced the flavour of the cooked meat. Generations, after bunching into tribes, began venturing into uncharted territories and established their own colonies during their migrations.

Historians and archaeologists have long contemplated the significance of this communal existence in primitive dwellings as the dawn of society. However, Rousseau, in *The Social Contract*, posited that society begins one step earlier. He suggests that a natural family – a father, mother, and children – forms the primal societal unit unwittingly. Children are tied to their parents for their survival. But, just like how ancient humans broke off from their original group to settle on their own, children too break off from their parents.

Nevertheless, exceptions always exist for every rule, and so it does in this case as well. There are cases of enduring families even today, irrespective of the differences that may occur in between various family members. This unity results more from individuals choosing to sustain relationships than from the mere influence of nature. On the flip side, societal conventions are thrown to the wind when some individuals do not think twice while breaking apart a picture-perfect family. How does this happen, one might ask? Well, the answer to that is individual liberty arising from humankind's intrinsic nature.

Human behaviour is predominantly governed by self-preservation. In moments of push coming to shove, personal concerns often eclipse the considerations of the larger society in general. It happens when one attains the age when one can think critically and independently. At this juncture, individuals assess whether their actions ensure sustained survival and if the answer is a 'yes', then they would not think twice to act on their thoughts.

Rousseau's analogy of family-to-society remains pertinent to answer this quandary. In a family, the father is perceived as the leader of the society, while the children are akin to the people residing in it. Both the leader and the people have the free will to do as they please and relinquish their liberties only if it is beneficial to them. There is one succinct difference, though. In a family, a father's love for his children is reciprocal to the amount of concern he bestows on his children. On the contrary, in a society, the leader derives satisfaction from ruling the masses to make up for the indifference towards his citizens.

Philosophers like Grotius challenged the belief that authority in a society exists solely for the benefit of its inhabitants. Grotius questioned how slavery came into being if universal welfare underscored society's genesis? Was this rationale the guiding force for emperors like Caligula, who compared themselves to gods? One thing is for true; the mere presence of authority has splintered people into different herds, much like cattle or sheep, and each herd has been left to fend for itself, being led by the strongest of the herd as a leader.

If society's inception was aimed at enriching the lives of those living within it, then why do some break away from the group? One snippet of information which may prove valuable is the deep-rooted self-consciousness that our human brains are hard wired with. You see, over the course of evolving from apes, the human mind began to think in a logical manner. Individuals began to recognize that if a particular line of thought was not adhering to what they believed, then consensus was it wasn't the right way to proceed.

When this happens in a society, there would always be a multitude of individuals who would not be willing to accept the authority imposed on them. So, it is only logical for these individuals to group together and splinter away. In this case, the individual liberties of both groups are maintained and both groups are expected to live in harmony unless they clash with each other down the line due to their ultimately differing beliefs.

The famed Greek philosopher Aristotle said that all men are not born equal; some are born to be ruled, while others are born to rule over the masses. While his statement is partly true in today's world, Aristotle's way of thinking was slightly flawed. Essentially, Aristotle's statement is more of correlation is equal to causation, which, as we know today, is not at all true. For example, every individual who is born in slavery is condemned to remain in slavery. That much adheres to Aristotle's philosophy. However, what he fails to understand is that slaves still retain individual rational thinking, which leads to thoughts of escaping servitude, and the desire to become rich. The Aristotlean philosophy doesn't account for any of this.

This is where our rational thinking comes into play. Slavery exists as an anathema to nature. Those who were made slaves were coerced into being so. However, if someone chose to continue to being a slave, then it is only due to their own cowardice rather than a lack of opportunity. There have been so many accounts of daring slave escapades right from ancient times to as recently as the twentieth century slave trade during the Ottoman Empire. But why did so few escape, while the rest continued with their miserable lives?

It is a classic case of falling into a rut and failing to come out of it. In today's fast-paced life, it is very easy to fall into the inertia of working from 9 to 5, and lounge about doing nothing afterwards. But it takes courage and perseverance to build a comprehensive regimen that encompasses all aspects of life viz. exercising, travelling, meeting new people, and starting a family. The slaves were often victims of their own miserable thoughts. They were of the opinion that while remaining slaves; they were fed thrice a day, and had a roof over their heads. They were terrified into thinking of the horrors of the outside world. Those who escaped captivity chose to think otherwise. They believed that any kind of life would be better than the hellhole they were currently subjected to. And hence, they mustered enough courage to break free from the clutches of bondage.

This then takes us back to the start: individual rational thinking can be directly attributed to the formation of civilized societies. We all arose from common ancestors and societies, and yet, the façade of societies around the world today bears no resemblance to the societies of the olden days. No one human can claim to be the sole leader of all of humankind. Though there have been attempts to deify Adam (of Adam and Eve) and his descendants as the true leaders of mankind, it has largely fallen flat. If Adam was indeed the first ever leader and all of mankind were his descendants, does that make everybody living today the leader of mankind?

A society exists only due to the presence of people living in it. And, a leader is considered to be a leader only if the citizens of a society continue to accept that person as a leader. Just like how a pride of lions chooses a new leader when the old one begins to fail in duties, humans would also not waste time in booting out the existing leader and ushering in a new one. After all, Tom Hanks was the sole leader on his island in the movie *Castaway*, only as long as he lived on the deserted island. And so was Robinson Crusoe in his own tale.

Social Organization and Hierarchies: Emergence of Chiefdoms and Early States

The advent of rational thinking in individuals in primitive societies led to the formation of newer communities. As these communities flourished, social hierarchies began to form. Some societies transitioned from loosely organized tribes to chiefdoms. These chiefdoms were characterized by hereditary leadership and a centralization of power. As populations grew, some of these chiefdoms developed into early states. These states were marked by even greater centralization of authority, establishment of formal laws, emergence of taxation on trade, and specialized labour, including artisans and bureaucrats. Urban centres began to emerge, which in turn fostered trade, cultural exchanges, and technological advancements.

Key Features of Early States

The earliest established states had a well-defined central authority figure. In the more primitive societies, this was the physically most powerful individual who was considered capable of leading the tribe. Over time, the advent of rational thinking led to people following a monarch or a ruler, who established control over their domain via more complex lines of thoughts in order to retain power, while giving the semblance of free will to the masses. Within these societies, a bureaucratic system emerged, which helped in the complex governance of taxation, law enforcement, and record-keeping.

People usually toed the line since they found this too complex and hence were willing to delegate it to a select group of individuals. Even so, philosophers in the past have theorized that this was primarily done for the concept of the 'greater good' over the comfort of the few. When urbanization of these societies happened, it came with advancements in political systems, economics, and cultural activities. Social stratification began and saw the emergence of distinct classes, such as priests, administrators, artisans, labourers, etc.

Factors that Contributed to the Rise in Society

Several factors contributed to the transition from hunter-gatherer societies to chiefdoms and early states. Historians have noted that the shift from hunting and gathering to sustained agriculture led to production of surplus food, which in turn enabled groups to support and develop non-food-producing classes.

Once societies were established over time, individuals began specializing in various tasks, such as agriculture, trade, and craftsmanship. This specialization of talents further fuelled the rise in social complexity. Finally, there was always the danger of internal conflicts, as well as external threats. This encouraged the development of a centralized power structure which then oversaw the rise of military factions.

Technological and Cultural Progress: Advancements and Exchange

As humans of similar line of thought settled in one place, they were able to dedicate more time to experimentation. This led to innovations in agriculture, tool-making, and architecture. Trade networks with other societies expanded, facilitating the exchange of goods, ideas, and cultural practices. The accumulation of knowledge and shared experiences paved the way for the emergence of art, religion, and complex belief systems.

Expansion of Knowledge

Technological advancements from societal humans ensured the exploration and consequently facilitating the understanding of the natural world in greater detail. The expansion of the knowledge base has led to more accurate explanations of natural phenomena, challenging and sometimes even replacing previously held beliefs. The best example of this is the origin of the heliocentric model of the solar system. Previously, it was believed that the earth was the centre of the solar system, while the other planets and the sun revolved around the earth. Over time, with sufficient advancements in science, it was found that it was the earth that revolved around the sun.

Rational Thinking, Critical Thinking, and Skepticism

As knowledge advanced, humans began to develop new tools and methods to solve problems. This emphasis on problem-solving contributed to the development of rational thinking. Through trial and error, experimentation, and the application of logical reasoning, humans in the earliest societies were able to develop innovative technologies. And then, this rational thinking was then disseminated over many generations through means such as word of mouth, scriptures, texts, and public discourses. This led to people questioning and critically evaluating any information.

Humanism and Individualism

Over time, when humans began advancing their technological prowess and the key aspects of critical thinking, it also inadvertently spawned a human-centric perspective that began to value individual contributions over group-based thoughts. Individuals began to focus on themselves. Thus began the two schools of thoughts of humanism and individualism.

In humanism, the intrinsic value and the potential of human beings are placed at the forefront as opposed to a solely religious or supernatural perspective. Most of the thoughts and actions with humanism as its foundation are majorly carried out for the collective good. In individualism, everything is about the individual. It emphasizes personal autonomy and encourages the pursuit of individual goals and desires.

***

Chapter 2

The Right of the Strongest

The person who is right, is the person who is the strongest, paradoxically in this case, it's the cowards who are the bravest, for they manage to impose their ideas on everyone else

—Paulo Coelho

In the previous chapter, a passing reference was made to the strongest of people gaining positions of authority when primitive societies first emerged into being. It is actually a philosophical notion that has been expressed and explored in various contexts, with particular relevance to Jean-Jacques Rousseau's *The Social Contract*. The idea posited by Rousseau delves into the dynamics of power, authority, and the formation of societies. This chapter aims to explore a bit more on the concept and its connection to Rousseau's work.

The concept of 'right of the strongest' essentially suggests that when there is an absence of established laws and norms of societal culture, absolute power and dominance is what determines what can be considered as right or just. The implication here is that the strongest individuals or groups of strong individuals tend to impose their will. This use of dominance can be traced back to our primitive ancestors and the time when they were just about forming groups, when physical strength and force often dictated the outcomes of conflicts and interactions.

Rousseau, in *The Social Contract*, examined the fundamental nature of human societies and mechanisms by which they are formed and governed. He states; 'the strongest individual is never indefinitely strong to be an authoritative figure, unless the individual transforms power into rights and sense of obedience to duty.' He says that the assumption of the right of the strongest is merely an irony, but had come to be established in principle because people ceded their liberties to live in a society with established conventions. This was, in fact, the nascent origins of the very first social contract. We can see that within the void of established laws, the 'right of the strongest' emerges as a shadowy force, and dominance becomes the arbiter of what is deemed just.

But is the so-called right of the strongest actually true? For the moment, let us assume it to be so, just as Rousseau did. We can quickly see that it spirals into an open-ended conflict of ideologies. Anybody with enough conviction in their own set of principles can muster enough courage and confidence to overthrow the ideas of the authority. And that is in part due to the existence of free will and individual liberties. Individual liberties in a society have given the legitimacy of disobeying orders with impunity. People who tend to act thus do so because they view their actions to be the strong; after all, those who are the strongest get the right to choose.

Over time, this newly acquired might is bound to perish. Then what would happen to the 'right of the strongest?' Rousseau states that, 'If one is compelled to obey by force, there is no need to obey from duty; and if one is no longer forced to obey, obligation is at an end.' By examining Rousseau's words in detail, we can see that the concept of 'rights' means nothing at all, and it doesn't add much to force.

The key detail in this treatise by Rousseau is that he encourages people to follow established norms in a civil manner, but not to do so when it violates individual liberties. So, he proposes that authority must arise from the consensus of the collective, rather than arbitrarily deciding on which individual or group of individuals are the strongest. To affirm his statement, Rousseau alludes to God, by saying; 'All power comes from God, but every disease comes from Him, too. Does it follow that we are prohibited from calling in a physician?'

Rousseau's line of thought is perfectly aligned for individuals to inculcate in today's world. Imagine a scenario where someone is happily driving a car back home. On the way, they come to a train crossing and pass it, only for the car's wheels to get stuck in between the rails. A train is barrelling down towards the car with absolute power, and the colossal size of the train in comparison to the car gives it physical authority as well. Now, should the occupant of the car simply sit inside and cede to the dominance of the train? Or should the occupant seek means of escaping the situation since it is not beneficial to them? This scenario is the perfect example that might is not always right. As individuals, we are not bound to obey any arbitrary power except for when the power is exercised for the greater good of the collective.

Slavery and the Right of the Strongest

Going back to the statement of might not being always be right; conventions remain the ultimate source of lawful authority among individuals in a society. In the previous chapter, we briefly dealt with the concept of slavery existing as a norm during the olden days. And here, we shall see in detail how this pertains to the concept of the right of the strongest. At this juncture, it is imperative to note Rousseau's statement; 'No man has any ultimate authority over his fellow men.'

Slavery traces its origins to times when rule of law and formal governance structures were absent. This spurred people in power to exert their dominance over the weaker sections of the masses, leading to subjugation and enslavement of individuals or groups. In respect to the right of the strongest, those who had the physical power to do so often imposed their dominance over the weak without any legal or moral restraint.

Rousseau asks a very pertinent question in *The Social Contract* – if an individual willingly or unwillingly cedes their freedom to become the slave to a master, why should societies not cede their freedoms to their leader? The pertinent word here is 'cede'. The word 'cede' refers to giving up or selling one's rights or the rights of things or an area.

When a man becomes a slave, he cedes his liberties on the basis that his basic subsistence would be met by the master. Or so he thinks, according to Rousseau. They do not yet understand the horrors that await them in the form of slavery. Rousseau drills in deeper to ask if it would be prudent for a whole society to cede their rights. An analogy is made to a fictional kingdom where the people of the kingdom have ceded their rights to the king. The king provides his people with subsistence and draws his own subsistence from the people; the only difference being a king doesn't live a small life. If the citizens of this kingdom cede their rights, would they be comfortable in ceding their properties, their assets, and even their souls?

A tyrannical leader is said to exercise their authority on the basis of securing tranquility for their subjects. But by doing so, what is it that they gain in the process? Absolute power causes corruption of the mind. Corrupted ambitions of a despot can lead to incessant wars on people being presided over. Then there's the greed and vexations of administration over the populace. Rousseau puts it aptly by saying: 'Men live in tranquility within dungeons. But are they really contented in that setting?' History is full of mythological stories, like the Ancient Greeks, Romans, and even Indian mythologies, that allude to Rousseau's statement, wherein an all-powerful monster had been entrapped by people for temporary tranquil, but it was only a matter of time till they were devoured as well.

It needs to be stated that an individual may cede their own rights for next to nothing. It also needs to be stated that this concept is illogical. No one in their right mind would cede wilful control over their liberties. It inevitably happens due to coercion.

Note, slavery doesn't always mean paying obeisance to a master. There are many kinds of slavery that exist in today's world. Many of us are unwittingly slaves to technology. All it takes to perceive this is a glance at the sidewalk, where one can see people of all ages glued to the screens of their mobile phones. If only they had the rationality to deal with the harmful consequences of technology, then we might see another renaissance period.

Despite the absurdity of it all, even if an individual does cede wilful control, they simply cannot do so for their peers or loved ones. Rousseau states that, 'every man is born of a free will; their liberties belong to them and no one can cede those liberties except them themselves.'

Let us now go back to Rousseau's original definition of society, where he draws parallels to a family. A father can establish preconditions for the preservation and welfare of his children. But this is logically possible only until the children attain the age of rational thinking.

Once the children begin thinking for themselves, they can question whether the preconditions irrevocably and unconditionally impinge on their liberties as free souls. If it does, then the newest entrants to the logical thinkers' club can deem it contrary to nature and refuse to abide by them anymore.

Similarly, as humans with the power of rational thinking, we need to exercise our rights to judge the legitimacy of authority whenever it is deemed as harmful, and replace the authority with one that closely aligns to the greater good of the collective. Thereby, any arbitrariness would be removed. Thereby, any aspect of being a slave or promoting conditions for imposition of slavery would also be removed.

Individual Liberties

An individual's liberty to do things at one's own bidding is what comprises the essence of humanity. Rousseau states that 'to renounce this liberty is akin to renouncing one's humanness.' When an individual falls into the trap of slavery (in any form or kind), they also renounce their rights and duties of humanity. Rousseau states that there is no compensation for people who renounce everything human and are entrapped by slavery.

It is often stated that 'morality is merely the lack of opportunity.' An unscrupulous person waits for the correct opportunity to let go of their morals in order to impose their dominance over the weak. And the weak make use of the opportunity to let go of their morals to get trapped. Letting go of the civil liberties of an individual, or by an individual, is something that goes against nature. Therefore, a social convention where one side is expected to infinitely obey the authority or the thrall of the other side is to be considered meaningless and contradictory.

Rousseau beautifully elucidates this contradiction in *The Social Contract.* If an individual becomes the slave of another individual, then the master has no obligations towards the slave. A master would own everything of the slave, hence the term 'slave', and therefore the rights of the slave as well. So would the master use his own rights (in the form of the slaves) against themselves?

This is where individual liberties take precedence over everything else. An individual is free to purchase life at the cost of personal freedom, but it must be in a form that would be beneficial to both parties. For example, an individual is free to cede civil liberties in a housing society. The homeowner imposes rent, and the individual gets a place to stay in. However, it must not be the case where the homeowner unjustly treats the tenant to give up control of their personal lives. That is impinging on the liberties of an individual.

War and Slavery

Since ancient times, the more infamous concept of slavery was born during times of war. The victorious party more often than not imposed their conditions on the vanquished. However, it needs to be cleared that the two are mutually exclusive of each other. While it is true that most of slavery was born due to war, it wasn't the main underlying cause. Humans, if left in a group, do not consider the other person as enemies to the extent it leads to war. Sure, competitions arise, but more often than not, this is restricted to one-upmanship rather than physical duels.

And yet, laws that were established during the state of war between man and man, or state and state, or ideology and ideology, led to the rise of slavery. Rousseau states in *The Social Contract* that most private duels do not constitute a state of war. By that logic, even battle with one's own inner demons cannot be construed as a state of war. Most of the laws that enabled slavery were as a direct result of the abuse of existing authority.

It can be stated, as per Rousseau's words, that war can only exist between one state and the other, wherein individuals become accidental enemies. In the war of State A vs. State B, citizens become soldiers to play the part of defending the homeland. State A cannot be the enemy of the citizen of State B. It would be impossible to do so since it would be impossible to claim such a relationship to cause enmity in the first place.

Sadly, even in today's so-called civilized age, we often see State A declaring war against the citizens of State B. These declarations of war are merely a power play to establish dominance. This only makes State A more akin to being a pirate for unlawfully robbing, slaying, or detaining citizens of a sovereign nation without declaring war against the government of that sovereign nation. And it is through this form of 'piracy', did most of the ancient slave trade occur.

Rousseau states that a slave acquired through war of any means is not obliged to obey a 'master' at any time, unless the individual who has ceded liberties is compelled to do so. Though conquest establishes the right to assert dominance, this right doesn't entail control over the liberties of the vanquished individual. By taking control of a slave, the victor has not done themselves any good as a slave will always be at war with the master. And, any societal convention that establishes such a system unto law doesn't stop war but ensures its continuance.

Need for Societal Convention

Slavery will always exist, unless there are well-established conventions to prevent it from happening altogether. Individuals can be subjugated in one form or the other, but when people get into a collective, the rationality of the collective is sure to overcome such subjugation (though with exceptions like being slaves to technology, as mentioned before). When an individual is subjugated, it is a slave answering to one master. But an entire horde of people is almost guaranteed not to bend to a tyrannical overlord.

When people accede themselves to a sovereign, Rousseau states that it is a civil act and needs public deliberation. But before this public discourse on how to elect a leader, it must be known what makes a group of people as people. That would set precedence for establishing norms that don't violate anybody's civil rights.

And if these civil rights did not exist, the minority would be subjugated by the wishes of the majority. In a classic example, there might be a thousand people who wish for bacon as their everyday breakfast meal, and therefore want to enact a law that would provide free bacon for everyone. However, there might be ten people who want avocado toast instead. So how would the laws established by the thousand would impact the lives of the ten? Unfortunately, or fortunately, the plurality of votes is generally established by conventions. And it more often than not presupposes unanimity, according to Rousseau.

***

Chapter 3

The Social Contract

> *The social contract is the act by which individuals mutually agree to create a government, surrendering some of their liberties and agreeing to obey the rules established by that government*
>
> —John Locke

Up until now, we have seen the origin of primitive societies and how the right of the strongest came about in establishing a hierarchical succession. However, we have also seen the concept of rational thinking of people in accepting the leadership thrust upon them. Now, why does an individual willingly cede their liberties to an unknown outsider to rule them? This is where the idea of the social contract came into being. It takes us on a journey to explore the origins of societies and governments, at a time before rules, laws, and organized systems existed – a time often referred to as the 'state of nature' by various philosophers. This hypothetical state of nature envisions a world where individuals lived independently, driven by their instincts and desires. In this state, there were no laws to follow, no authorities to enforce order, and no structured means of resolving conflicts.

In the state of nature, individuals were free to act according to their own will, without external limitations. While this freedom might sound appealing, it also brought about its fair share of challenges. Without clear rules, clashes of interest arose among individuals. Inevitably, conflicts followed, leading to an atmosphere of insecurity and constant tension in nascent societies.

In this chaotic environment, the absence of a common authority meant that individuals had to rely solely on their own strength to protect themselves and their possessions. This need for self-defence and protection often led to a cycle of violence, where might determined right; hence, the rise of the right of the strongest.

Amidst the tumultuous period, the rational human mind began to pose a natural question: How could individuals transition from this state of nature to a more organized and secure society? The idea was a nifty one. A group of individuals got together and thought, let's create a contract with the authority. We shall willingly surrender certain personal liberties, but the authority has to guarantee certain benefits of collective living. It was this voluntary agreement that aimed to establish a society where individuals could enjoy a more stable and harmonious existence.

The social contract was not developed overnight. Individuals who wanted to have a contract with the authorities recognized that, while the state of nature offered freedom, it lacked the assurance of security and cooperation. By entering into a social contract, individuals could create a framework that would enable them to coexist peacefully. They could establish rules that would protect their rights and ensure that disputes were resolved fairly. This transition required individuals to set aside some of their personal liberties.

The social contract can be viewed as a foundational pact that forms the basis of many modern societies. Over time, it marked a significant shift from an anarchic state of nature to a more ordered and regulated existence. Through the establishment of a social contract, individuals collectively decided to create a government that would have the authority to create and enforce laws. This authority, derived from the consent of the governed, aimed at safeguarding the rights and interests of all members of society. In hindsight, one can also say that the social contract was one of the pillars of modern-day democracy, wherein the adage of 'for the people, of the people, and by the people' came into being.

Problems Addressed by a Social Contract

When mankind is faced with self-preservation, individuals come to realize that they cannot conjure something new out of thin air. They can only control what is given to them. This was how the earliest proponents of the social contract came about to giving up their individual freedoms. In his treatise, *The Social Contract*, Rousseau states that the social contract addresses a major issue – to create a way for a group to work together to keep everyone safe and protect each person's belongings, allowing everyone to join in while still making their own choices, staying as free as they were before.

By drawing up a social contract to address this issue, individuals also modified the clauses of the contract in such a way that if any act was to be counterintuitive or modified, then the clauses and the contract itself would be rendered pointless and ineffectual. Therefore, individuals in a society tacitly accepted the terms of authority to live in a society until the time the contract was violated. Rousseau states that an individual would do well to take back their natural liberties when the social contract was violated.

While oftentimes this is mistaken for rebellion, let us not forget what rebellion actually is. Rebellion is the thunderous echo of individual voices that refuses to be silenced by the chains of conformity. When individuals are unjustly curtailed by those in power, it often leads to dissent, since this was not a part of the deal when they voluntarily renounced their conventional liberty.

Clauses of the Social Contract

Every contract that we sign today is bookended by a multitude of clauses. Likewise, Rousseau states that the social contract also has clauses of it. When the clauses of the social contract are understood correctly, it can be simplified into one single clause: Total ceding of individual rights so that the situation is the same for one and all. When conditions are equal for all, then no one would think of making themselves a burden upon others.

Furthermore, when individuals cede their rights without reserve, then the social contract can be said to be perfect, thereby not necessitating an individual to seek extra validation. If individuals retained any rights, then there wouldn't be any common superior to mediate issues that cropped up between individuals of the society, since every individual would then claim to be a superior judge of their situations. This would then again take society back to the state of nature.

Therefore, the calls for the need of a 'republic' or a 'political' body, as opposed to just a 'city' or 'town' formed by individuals of society. When this political body is passive, it is termed as the 'state', since the state is usually elected by its citizens. However, when the political body is active, i.e. derived from a hierarchical transfer of power, it is referred to as the 'sovereign'. When different political bodies are compared with each other, the term 'power' is used to denote the differences in governing bodies.

With regards to individuals, they can collectively be called as 'citizens' if they partake in sovereign power and 'subjects' if they follow the laws of the state. In today's world, these terminologies are often interchangeably used, but historians have concurred that these are independent and unique terminologies which denote the type of social contract that they have undertaken. When misrepresenting the terminologies, people often overlook the fact that it is the citizens that make a city. Kingdoms in the past have suffered terrible fates because they overlooked this very fact and neglected the citizens. Similarly, many governments around the world today continue to make the same mistake.

Rebellion

Rebellion is a potent force within the framework of the social contract. It emerged as a complex response of a single individual, or in most cases a group of like-minded individuals, to the intricate balance between individual rights and the authority of a governing body. As societies progressed and established systems of governance through the social contract, an unspoken pact materialized. This tacit agreement dictated that the government would safeguard the rights and interests of its citizens, contingent upon the citizens' compliance with the government's laws.

However, in the annals of history, instances have arisen where the government intended to be a protector of rights, transforms into an entity that suppresses and infringes upon those very rights. In these junctures, acts of rebellion arise. Rebellion is a multifaceted phenomenon rooted in the tension between the duty to uphold the social contract and the right to resist when that contract is transgressed.

Rebellion can manifest as a poignant response to an unjust government; a mechanism through which individuals can reclaim their voice when it's stifled. It's a reminder that the social contract is a reciprocal agreement; the government's legitimacy rests upon its adherence to its obligations just as much as citizens' compliance does. When this balance is disrupted and the scales tip towards oppression, rebellion emerges as a counterbalance.

However, rebellion is not a step taken lightly. It's a course of action fraught with complexities, as it raises questions about the scope of resistance, the means employed, and the potential consequences. The act of rebellion holds a mirror to a society's moral and ethical fabric.

Rebellion's role within the social contract is not only as a reactionary force but also as a catalyst for societal evolution. It forces governments to reckon with their responsibilities, recalibrate their actions, and address the grievances that ignited the flames of resistance. It reminds citizens that the social contract is a living document, one that must be upheld not just by the government but also by the people.

Recklessness of Rebellion

It has already been established by now that rebellion involves challenging established norms and institutions. However, this very disruption can lead to a chain reaction of events that spiral beyond control. Rebellion, by its nature, is disruptive and breeds chaos and instability.

One of the most reckless aspects of rebellion is the associated violence and loss of life. As individuals rise up against authority, clashes between rebels and those tasked with maintaining order become increasingly likely. What might start as a peaceful protest often swiftly escalates into a violent confrontation. The recklessness of rebellion lies in the uncertainty of how far this violence might extend and the irreversible damage it can inflict upon societies.

Furthermore, rebellion often occurs within a context where emotions are heightened, and polarization is rampant. While it might appear as a unified front against a common oppressor, the reality is often more nuanced. Internal divisions among the rebels themselves can lead to splintering factions. This fragmentation can weaken the rebellion's overall impact and create power vacuums that are exploited by opportunistic forces.

The aftermath of a rebellion can be just as tumultuous as the act itself. The sudden removal of a governing authority, even if perceived as tyrannical, leads to a power vacuum that is not easily filled. The transition to a new order is rarely smooth, and it inevitably results in further power struggles, instability, and prolonged periods of uncertainty. The very act intended to address grievances might inadvertently lead to a situation that is far worse.

The destruction that often accompanies rebellions can set back progress for years, if not decades. The economic ramifications of rebellion can leave societies struggling to rebuild and recover. Concomitantly, the divisions sown during a rebellion can linger long after the dust has settled, leaving societies fractured and struggling to reconcile differences. While rebellion may begin with a noble cause and the hope of positive change, the reality is that the trajectory of rebellion is often uncertain. It's a risky venture that can unleash forces beyond anyone's control.

Let's imagine that the society is shrunk to the size of a classroom of thirty students. The teacher is the ultimate authority of the classroom, and the students have temporarily ceded their personal liberties in return for the teacher to partake in knowledge dissemination. Now, the unspoken rule is that as long as the teacher teaches something of use to the students, is interesting, and it makes them involved, the students are happy to comply with the authority of the teacher. Here, the students have signed the social contract with the teacher. Everything is in harmony.

Over the course of the academic year, some students begin to realize that the teacher's style is slowly pandering only to the brightest of minds. This irks the students who are of average academic outlook. They band together and begin misbehaving in class. This is considered to be an act of rebellion. However, since all actions have consequences, the teacher imposes their authority to suspend the miscreant students. This creates disharmony in the classroom as to why so many students are suspended.

Inadvertently, many people are involved. The parents of the suspended students want to take action against the teacher and instigate their children to continue with their miscreant behaviour. The classroom is now split into two halves of those believing in the teacher and those opposing the teacher. Emotions flare up, tempers boil over. Classes get disrupted and the rebelling students begin to resort to violence to make their voices heard. This is the polarization which happens in society as well when rebellion happens.

Soon, the teacher is removed and replaced with a new one in order to quell the disharmony of the classroom. But the end result is even worse. The new teacher proves to be inept at handling the already frayed tempers of the students. This is the power void left behind due to recklessness of rebellion.

The key takeaway here is that it is okay to be a rebel, but it is not okay to rebel and disrupt the life of others in the society. Grievances can be got across in a more peaceful manner. Rational thinking can ensure that a sane line of dialogue is maintained between opposing parties. Rebelling parties can use tact and logic, while authorities can use restraint to leverage their semi-autonomous power and get things done. While history has shown that rebellion can indeed bring about transformation, it's essential to carefully weigh the risks and potential consequences before embracing the path of upheaval.

Influence of the Social Contract

At its core, the social contract encourages individuals to consider the balance between their individual freedoms and the needs of the community. This duality is encapsulated in the notion that while individuals surrender certain liberties for the sake of collective security, they also retain essential rights. This balance prompts individuals to reflect on the limits of their actions and the implications of their decisions on others. It fosters a sense of responsibility and encourages individuals to see themselves as active participants in the social fabric.

Furthermore, the social contract kindled a deeper exploration of ethical and moral considerations. The idea that individuals voluntarily enter into an agreement to abide by certain rules encourages individuals to question not only what is legal but also what is just and fair. This introspection has led to the development of philosophical and ethical discussions about the nature of rights, justice, and the common good.

In shaping individual thinking, the social contract has also prompted people to consider the essence of citizenship. It has spurred conversations about civic duties, the role of active engagement in governance, and the idea that individuals have a stake in the well-being of their communities, thus fulfilling responsibilities, such as voting, paying taxes, and participating in civil discourse.

In the realm of personal liberty, the social contract has led individuals to reflect on the nature of their freedoms and the boundaries that define them. The contract acknowledges that, while individuals may relinquish certain freedoms for societal order, they retain fundamental rights that cannot be infringed upon, contributing to discussions about privacy, individual autonomy, and the role of the state in safeguarding personal freedoms.

As societies evolve and encounter new challenges, the social contract continues to serve as a touchstone for addressing complex issues. It encourages individuals to think critically about the social order, the legitimacy of authority, and the responsibilities of both citizens and governments. This enduring influence speaks to the relevance of the social contract as a guiding principle in shaping societies and fostering thoughtful, engaged individuals.

In the words of this newfound understanding, the social contract reminds us that while we come together for mutual protection, we remain bound by the threads of shared responsibility and the tapestry of collective progress.

Chapter 4

The Sovereign

The sovereign is like a guiding star which helps to steer the ship of society through the vast sea of challenges and chart a course towards common good.

In the clauses of the social contract in the previous chapter, terminologies like the sovereign, state, citizens etc. were all elaborated for better understanding. Rousseau, in his treatise *The Social Contract*, states that associated individuals in a social contract are engaged in a reciprocal arrangement between themselves and the general public. There is also a double relationship at play here, that is, the relationship between a sovereign towards the individuals of their realm, as well as the relationship between members of the state towards the sovereign.

As with all contracts, a social contract is also up for public deliberations, in this case, binding of the subjects to the sovereign. However, Rousseau states that the maxim of civil laws would be applicable to the sovereign itself, since a sovereign cannot pass a law which is contrary to the nature of a political body; a law which by definition a sovereign themselves cannot transgress. It is to be noted that during times of emergencies to a sovereign's realm, the sovereign is empowered to take decisions for the greater good of the society.

At its core, the sovereign is a compelling idea. Imagine a group of individuals, diverse in every way, coming together to form a unified body that is empowered to make collective decisions for the common good. This collective entity, also known as the sovereign, represents the general will of the people of the society. Rousseau believed that the social contract, through which individuals willingly surrender some of their personal freedom to the sovereign, is the very foundation of civil society; one that is always aimed towards the greater good.

When sovereignty is reduced to nothing but exercising the general will of the populace, then the concept of sovereignty becomes indelible. It becomes a collective being than can be represented only by itself. The power of the sovereign can then be transmitted from one individual or group of individuals, but not the will of the sovereign itself. As a result, the sovereign can dream of wanting what a certain individual desires at the moment. However, the sovereign cannot thus dream of wanting what an individual may dream of in the future. When people abide by the latter dream of the sovereign, then it falls into the realms of absurdity and the concept of the sovereign is lost. This leads to destruction of the political body, thereby dissolving the concept of a sovereign.

The sovereign is also considered to be indivisible in a society for the same reason it is indelible. When the collective will of people wants a governing authority, the sovereign is inevitably born into being as an undivided figure. If the sovereign devolves into passing edicts that console only a group of individuals, then that edict is no longer for the general good. However, the politicians of the current day cannot enforce the core tenets of sovereignty.

Instead, they divide it into legislative and executive powers. Taxation, justice, war, internal and external affairs – all are either conflated for easier understanding of the people or divided for easier enactment of laws pertaining to these. Imagine

Dr Frankenstein's monster, which was built from the parts of various dead human beings and brought to life. That is precisely how we end up viewing authority these days. The head, for example, relates to the governing bodies of the government. The hands relate to the defence ministry. The feet relate to the transportation body, while the torso with its various organs represents the internal and external affairs divisions.

Our politicians have become adept in the skill of pulling wool over our eyes to make the sovereign almost unrecognizable to the people. A fantastic authoritative being has been dismembered by almost magic worthy skills and the parts have been recombined in the most unlikely of ways to represent the body of authority. This is also partly undertaken to ensure a high enough entry barrier to dissuade anybody else from even dreaming of power.

For example, declaring war and restoring peace is viewed by the politicians as an absolute right of the authoritative body and the people have no say. They are reduced to mere pawns. There are no laws in place which state what constitutes an act of war, and what would constitute the restoration of peace. In fact, there is no law which states that every citizen of the country should be consulted before declaring war. These obscure facets may lead it to seem that sovereignty is indeed divided. But we couldn't be farther from the truth. A sovereign figure is indeed undivided and the parts of authority that seem disparate all bow down to the supreme will of rights and functions.

Influence on Society

So, how does the sovereign influence society? Think of it as the steering mechanism of a ship called the 'State'. The sovereign, as the embodiment of the general will, determines the direction in which the state sails by providing it clear guidance. The sovereign decides on laws, policies, and actions. In a well-functioning society, this power is exercised with the welfare of all in mind, though not always all people are impacted by the enacted policies.

Picture a scenario where the sovereign, representing the people's collective will, decides to build a new school in a neighbourhood. This decision reflects the shared belief between the sovereign and people that education is essential for the community's betterment. In this example, the sovereign shapes the members of the society, ultimately enhancing the quality of life for its members. In due course of time, the educated members themselves could aspire to become the sovereign through displays of rational thinking.

In this manner, when the sovereign enacts certain decisions, it is always done keeping in mind the larger interests of the society. However, certain policies may not end up benefitting the society in general. For example, the vast and intricate roadway system in the US was conceived by its leaders to boost the sales of the bourgeoning car industry. However, in due course of time, public transportation was neglected to such an extent that people who could not afford a car found it difficult to travel from place to place. This is a prime example of a decision taken by the authorities on the fly, leading to long term negative consequences.

Influence on Individual Thinking

The sovereign not only influences the way a society thinks and acts, it also influences how individuals think and act. When people unite under the banner of the sovereign, they become part of a broader community with shared interests and aspirations. That is not to say that under the collective identity, an individual is forbidden from having thoughts and aspirations of their own. It is just that their larger interests gel with the other members of the society that have pledged allegiance to the sovereign.

For example, there is a person living in a society where the sovereign places great value on environmental conservation. Over time, this individual is likely to appreciate the importance of preserving nature for future generations. The sovereign's emphasis on environmentalism doesn't merely affect policies; it also moulds the values of its citizens. Similarly, if a sovereign prioritizes rampant development without placing value on the surrounding environment, it is highly likely that the individual living in such a society would not care two hoots about the environment.

The Balance of Rights and Duties

In his treatise, Rousseau argues that the social contract is not a one-sided agreement. While individuals surrender certain freedoms to the sovereign, they gain something invaluable in return: civil rights and the protection of their natural rights.

Let us consider the right to property. In a state governed by the sovereign, this right is protected from infringement by others. If someone attempts to unjustly seize another's property, the sovereign intervenes either through laws or through use of force, thereby ensuring that justice is served. By doing so, the sovereign ensures that individual rights are protected while the sovereign themselves perform their expected duties. This balance of rights and duties establishes a sense of security and fairness within individuals of the society.

Laws and Regulations

The sovereign's influence extends to the creation and enforcement of laws and regulations to govern the individuals in a society. Any civil society is marked by the presence of good governance laws, and they are a manifestation of the collective will. They define what is acceptable behaviour and ensure order and harmony in the society. Laws, in essence, act as a moral compass for individuals. And the sovereign, by providing these laws, ensures that their citizens have a moral compass.

Let's take an example of traffic regulations, which is much more in tune with what is happening in today's world. When the sovereign (in this case authorities) establishes rules like stopping at red lights and yielding to pedestrians, it's not just about preventing chaos on the roads; it's a reflection of the collective desire for safety and order. Individuals contribute to the well-being of the community when they adhere to these laws. On the other hand, in a society with absence of laws of good governance, it can be said that the society is doomed to fail since individual thinking goes haywire and does not adhere to any set system for the greater good of society.

Challenge to the Individual Will

While the sovereign's influence may seem pervasive and come off as overbearing at times, it is definitely not absolute. In *The Social Contract*, Rousseau acknowledges that the general will of the populace could potentially clash with individual desires. In such cases, individuals might be compelled to follow the general will. This tension between personal desires and the compulsion to follow orders for the collective good is a fundamental challenge posed by the decisions of the sovereign.

Imagine a scenario where the sovereign decides to impose higher taxes to fund public healthcare. While this decision is beneficial for the society at large, it may end up burdening individuals with greater financial obligations. Some people might have additional unforeseen expenses which may not leave them with enough money to pay for healthcare premiums. Here, the clash between personal financial interests and the collective well-being emerges. It's a dilemma that individuals in a civil society often face, prompting them to weigh their personal desires against the decisions for the greater good taken by the sovereign.

The Evolution of the Sovereign

By now, it may be realized that the concept of the sovereign is not a static one. It is one that evolves with societal changes. The sovereign must be adaptable to address new challenges and priorities of the society as and when it arises. When societies progress, so does the sovereign.

There was once a time during the colonial period of human history when women were not considered for suffrage by the sovereign. Over time, women in different empires and lands collectively began to bargain for their right to vote, given that they were anyway being involved in different streams of work where men were their colleagues. This was long contested by the sovereigns of the respective realms till it all changed in the early twentieth century after women contributed a lot to the war effort during the First World War. Sovereigns began enacting policies that promoted equal opportunities and voting rights for women. This evolution highlights the dynamic nature of the sovereign and its responsiveness to the evolving consciousness of society.

Limits of Sovereign Power: Striking a Balance for Justice

In the realm of governing a society, the idea of sovereign power holds immense significance. It's like the engine that drives the societal train. Yet, just like any engine, it needs boundaries. Imagine a car without brakes – it might speed ahead, but disaster would be inevitable. Similarly, the idea of limits on sovereign power is crucial to prevent the train of society from derailing.

Rousseau, in *The Social Contract*, gave us insights into this idea in simple terms. He believed that while sovereign power is necessary, it should have boundaries. It can be compared to 'fences that prevent power from trampling on people's rights' for want of a better analogy. In his work *The Social Contract*, he illustrated that the social contract – the agreement where we all live together under certain rules – is like a promise. We agree to follow the rules set by the sovereign, and in return, the sovereign promises to protect our rights.

Power Pact: The General Will

The concept of the general will is the compass guiding the ship of society. Think of it as a GPS programmed with the collective desires of the people. The sovereign's power is supposed to be in line with this general will. But here's the catch – the general will isn't about a majority overpowering a minority. Rousseau clarified that it should represent the overall good of the society. 'The sovereign's power should serve the greater good and not just some people's interests.'

Laws for the Sovereign

Ever wonder why we have laws? Well, they're like the safety nets in a circus act, there to catch you if you fall. In a society, laws are the tools to ensure that the sovereign doesn't cross its limits. They're the concrete expressions of the social contract. Rousseau believed that laws should be fair and just, reflecting the common interest. When the sovereign goes beyond these rules, it risks going beyond its authority.

One of the most important aspects of limiting sovereign power is safeguarding individual freedom. It's like saying, 'You can drive your car when you want and where you want it, but you can't run over other people.' This means that while the sovereign can make rules, it can't infringe on our basic rights like freedom or property. Moreover, the will of the people can also help in enforcing the limits to which a sovereign exercises their power. Citizens must not just be limited to being passengers on a cruise ship, but must take part in steering the helm so that a sovereign's absolute authority is kept in check.

Chapter 5

The Civil State

Civilization thrives in the embrace of the civil state, where the collective wisdom of the people builds bridges to a brighter future, and the rule of law guides us through the labyrinth of progress.

Humanity is said to have undergone a radical transformation when they evolved from the state of nature to a more civilized society. Until the formation of a civil society, humanity as a whole was more engrossed with one's own thoughts and inclinations. When the voice of duty and the long arm of the law prevailed over individualistic ambitions and impulses, people began to understand that they would need to act in accordance to established principles and listen to their rational mind.

In a civil state, it is generally noted that individuals give up their advantages they gained from nature. But, in return, individuals acquire even greater advantages by doing so. In a civil state, an individual is encouraged to use and develop their mental faculties. Their emotional faculties are enhanced, and they are empowered to connect with their soul. Humanity as a whole begins to feel that a civil state is a blessing for them in disguise and a one that transformed them from a primal feral being to a more intelligent species.

Drilling down to the barest of concepts, when an individual enters into a social contract for being in a civil state, the only thing the individual loses is the natural unfettered liberty to do anything that they might please. In return, what they gain is civil liberties and proprietary ownership of all things in their possession. At this juncture, it is crucial to delineate the differences between natural liberty and civil liberty.

Natural liberty is merely restricted to powers of an individual, such as the freedom to say what they want. In its purest form, natural liberty refers to the inherent rights that individuals possess simply by being human, independent of any social or governmental structures. The freedom to express thoughts, ideas, and opinions without fear of censorship or punishment is often considered a fundamental natural liberty. Natural liberty is the heartbeat of humanity, where the soul's desires dance freely in the symphony of existence.

Civil liberty, on the other hand, refers to those liberties which are restricted to the general will of the society in which the individual resides in, such as the right to vote. Civil liberties are the rights and freedoms that individuals enjoy within the framework of a structured society and its laws. The right to vote is a quintessential civil liberty that allows citizens to participate in the democratic process and have a say in the governance of their country. This right is protected by laws and regulations that ensure equal access to voting for all eligible citizens. Civil liberty is the compass that guides us through the labyrinth of society, granting us the freedom to navigate our paths and stand as architects of our collective destiny.

Throughout the course of history, the emergence of the civil state has left an indelible mark on human society and individual thinking. It has acted as a transformative force, reshaping the very fabric of our communities and influencing the way we perceive our roles in the world.

The Birth of the Civil State

Before delving into the effects, let's first understand what a civil state is. A civil state, in essence, is a society organized under a government that operates according to established laws and regulations. It's a place where order, justice, and the protection of individual rights prevail. The emergence of the civil state marked a significant departure from earlier forms of governance, where power often resided in the hands of a few (in most cases the strongest), and the rule of law was not the guiding principle (especially in the state of nature as described earlier).

In the dawn of the civil state, societies recognized that the unchecked power vested in a single ruler often led to chaos and the suppression of individual freedoms. The shift from this autocratic rule to a system governed by law can be compared to the transformation of a wild forest into a well-tended garden. This transition was not just a change in governance; it was a change in perspective.

The civil state was born out of a collective desire for a system that respects the dignity of each individual. It recognizes that every person has innate rights which cannot be violated without consequence. This principle can be likened to the foundation of a sturdy house – without a solid base of individual rights, the structure of society crumbles.

One of the key aspects during the birth of a civil state was the establishment of a social contract – a mutual agreement among individuals to form a cohesive society governed by rules and laws. This contract can be compared to a shared agreement among players in a game, determining the rules that everyone abides by for the game to proceed fairly.

Societal Evolution Through the Civil State

The advent of a civil state gave rise to a series of profound changes in society by acting as a framework on which progress was built. One of the most notable changes that a civil state brought upon was the establishment of laws that ensured equality for all while protecting individual rights. This, in turn, ensured a more just and inclusive society.

With a more inclusive society, the concept of citizenship evolved, wherein individuals became active participants in the affairs of the society. People weren't happy just being subjects of rulers. They wanted an equal say about what happened in their lives. In a way, citizenship helped people to shape the society in which they resided, with greater civic engagement by the people happened and a sense of shared responsibility.

Earlier, Rousseau alluded to the sovereign being a disparate object of authority made up of different moving parts, the establishment of the civil state led to division of power into the Legislative, Executive, and Judicial branches. This separation of power ensured that no one branch could assume ultimate authority over others. It ensured that decisions were taken via deliberations, thereby contributing to a more stable and accountable government.

The rule of law and protection of property rights ensured a flourishing commerce and trade system. A sense of confidence was instilled in people that led them to invest in innovations, under the knowledge that their investments would be rewarded if the innovations succeeded and protected if the innovations failed.

The rise of the civil state also fostered the growth of institutions like charities, arts, schools, and religious organizations. These institutions played a vital role in addressing the different needs of individuals in the society and promoted a sense of community in them.

Individual Rights and Liberties

It needs to be stressed that a society without the protection of individual rights is like a ship without a rudder – adrift and vulnerable amid the choppy waters of the high seas of life. People began to understand that they possessed inherent rights that no authority could arbitrarily take away. This newfound awareness led to a shift in thinking, where individuals started demanding their rights and resisting oppression. People began to understand that every individual had rights to their inherent worth and dignity.

The Civil State as a Guardian of Rights

The civil state acts as a protector of individual rights. It's like having a responsible friend who stands up for you when you're being treated unfairly. In a society without a civil state, your rights might be ignored or violated. But with the civil state in place, it's like having a rulebook that says, 'Every person's rights must be respected, no exceptions.'

With regards to freedom of expression, the civil state has certain laws that ensure the same. One can speak their mind, share their opinions, and even criticize those in power without fearing punishment. This empowerment is like having a voice that can be heard, no matter who you are. However, it is becoming increasingly rare these days, where those in power have started becoming skittish about the issue of freedom of expression and wish to curtail the extent to which an individual can speak about certain topics, such as efficacy of the government, criticizing other religions, etc.

The right to privacy has become a hot topic of contention in recent news. However, the civil state values your right to privacy. It's like having a locked diary that nobody can read without your permission. In a world without this protection, your personal information could be misused. But the civil state sets boundaries and rules, saying, 'Your personal life is your own, and no one can invade it without a good reason'.

The civil state ensures that everyone is treated equally. It's like making sure that all the players in a game have the same chances to win; everyone gets a fair shot, and nobody can discriminate against you based on things like your gender, race, or religion.

When the question of property arises, the civil state safeguards an individual's right to own property. It's like having a safe where your belongings are secure. In a state of nature, without this protection, an individual's property could be taken away without any rhyme or reason.

Within a civil state, all individuals are accorded rights to a fair trial if they're accused of something. It's like having a referee in a game. Without this protection, individuals can be punished without a proper chance to defend themselves. But the civil state guarantees that they have the right to be heard and treated justly.

Rational Discourse and Thinking

The civil state promoted rational discourse and critical thinking. In societies governed by the rule of law, decisions were made based on reason and evidence rather than arbitrary whims. The very laws that enabled this were themselves founded on rational thinking of the collective will. This emphasis on reason and enlightenment values spurred intellectual and scientific advancements.

In the bustling marketplace of ideas, the civil state stands as a beacon, inviting individuals to engage in rational discourse and embrace thoughtful thinking. It's like a garden where ideas bloom, nurtured by the principles of order, reason, and open dialogue. Let's delve into how the civil state has played a pivotal role in promoting rational discourse and thinking.

The civil state provides a fertile ground for reason to flourish. The civil state creates a safe space where reason can take centre stage. It's like a stage where different perspectives come together to perform a meaningful play. In a society without the civil state, ideas might be silenced by force or ignored. But the civil state sets the stage for rational discourse.

An open dialogue is said to be the bridge that connects different minds. When different individuals have differing viewpoints, they need a space where their views are likely to be heard, let alone be implemented. The civil state is more like a roundtable discussion where everyone seated at the table will be given a chance to speak.

When individuals make decisions on the basis of evidence rather than assumptions, one can truly say that the individual hails from a civil state. Imagine a jigsaw puzzle consisting of pieces that are put together to form a clear picture. Each piece of the puzzle is an individual mind that thinks about the collective good of the society. However, even if one individual digresses from this line of thought and begins to assume, rather than think on the basis of facts, then the jigsaw is incomplete.

In a civil state that promotes rational discourse, one can also witness a culture of curiosity, much like a hunt for hidden treasure. This is in direct contrast to a state of nature where people are often suppressed or discouraged from pursuing certain things. A true civil state is one where individuals are empowered to question, challenge assumptions, and contribute to the collective growth of knowledge.

When individuals of diverse backgrounds come together to form a collective, the presence of differing perspectives is inevitable. However, the civil state proves to be advantageous by recognizing that every viewpoint adds a unique colour to the mosaic that is the society, unlike in the state of nature, when often only a singular viewpoint is dominant, which would end up stifling the progress of the collective.

Tolerance and Pluralism

In today's diverse and interconnected world, the civil state plays a vital role in promoting tolerance and pluralism. These concepts are essential for creating harmonious and inclusive societies where people from various backgrounds can coexist peacefully.

So, how exactly does the civil state foster tolerance and pluralism? Tolerance, in the context of the civil state, means respecting and accepting the differences in people's beliefs, customs, and backgrounds. Just like how a garden is more beautiful when it has a variety of colourful flowers, a society is also more beautiful when it has people of diverse backgrounds. The civil state recognizes that diversity is not a problem to be solved, but strength to be celebrated.

Now, let's talk about pluralism. Pluralism is the idea that different groups and beliefs can peacefully coexist within a society. It's like having a big, diverse family where everyone respects each other's uniqueness. In the civil state, pluralism is not just a nice idea; it's a fundamental principle.

In the civil state, every person is granted equal rights and protections under the law. This means that no matter where you come from, what you believe, or who you love, you have the same legal rights as everyone else. This fosters tolerance by ensuring that no group is unfairly treated or discriminated against. Everyone has the right to practice religion or belief without interference. This freedom also means that one can choose not to follow any religion at all. It's like having the freedom to wear any type of clothes that one likes; it's a personal choice.

Education in the civil state is inclusive and respectful of diverse backgrounds. It teaches us about different cultures, histories, and perspectives. It's like having a buffet of knowledge, where you can try a little of everything. Inclusive education helps us understand and appreciate the richness of our world. Consequently, special care is taken to protect the rights of minority groups. These are groups of people who might be smaller or have less power. The civil state ensures that their voices are heard. It's like making sure that even the smallest fish in the pond has a safe place to swim.

Challenges and Ongoing Progress

The civil state, with its commitment to democracy, freedom, and equality, is a beacon of hope for creating just and inclusive societies. However, it's not all smooth sailing. The civil state faces its fair share of challenges, and one of the significant challenges is the erosion of democratic values. In some places, leaders are using their power to undermine democratic institutions and suppress opposition voices. This threatens the very essence of the civil state, which relies on democracy as its foundation.

Economic inequality continues to rise in many civil states. This means that while some people enjoy immense wealth, others struggle to make ends meet. Such inequality can undermine the idea of equal opportunities for all citizens, a core tenet of the civil state. Freedom of speech, a fundamental pillar of the civil state, faces challenges in an age of misinformation and online echo chambers. The spread of false information can manipulate public opinion and lead to division. Populist leaders sometimes appeal to the fears and prejudices of the masses, challenging the principles of inclusivity and tolerance. This can result in policies that weaken the civil state's pluralistic ideals.

On the flip side, many civil states are actively working to strengthen their democratic institutions. This includes reinforcing the independence of the judiciary, ensuring free and fair elections, and bolstering checks and balances on executive power. Efforts to address economic inequality are ongoing.

Civil states are also taking steps to combat misinformation and promote media literacy. Fact-checking initiatives, media literacy programmes, and responsible social media use are helping citizens become more discerning consumers of information. Many civil states are cooperating on the international stage to address global challenges. Climate change, pandemics, and human rights issues require collaborative efforts, and the civil state is a champion of such cooperation.

As citizens, we play a crucial role in upholding and strengthening the civil state by actively participating in democracy, advocating for equality, and promoting rational discourse and inclusivity. By addressing these challenges and continuing our efforts toward progress, we can ensure that the civil state remains a model for just and inclusive societies for generations to come.

Chapter 6

An Alternative Take on the Economy

The modern economy is fraught with challenges akin to the labours of Hercules. But with conviction, innovation, and determination, we can conquer every modern Lernean Hydra that may stand in our path.

We had dealt with the chaos of disorder during the formation of primitive societies and how harmony was ultimately formed via the social contract, presence of authority, and the birth of a civil state. Now, let us embark on a serene and contemplative journey through the labyrinth that is the economy. The best inspiration can be found amid the words of Henry David Thoreau in his book *Walden*, which he wrote during an introspective stay amid the peaceful Walden Woods. This nineteenth century text can serve as a timeless inspiration even for a twenty-first century audience that struggles in today's complex, interconnected, and an economy driven world.

In today's world, the modern economy is like a giant puzzle, where people and businesses work together to make life better. Imagine you want a new phone. You go online, pick one you like, and click a few buttons to buy it. That's how a lot of buying and selling happens nowadays – it's all digital. Money flows electronically, making things quick and easy. Things come from all over the globe. Your favourite shoes might be made in one country, while the parts for your computer come from another. This global trade helps give us lots of choices and keeps prices competitive.

Technology is the beating heart of the modern economy. Think of it as a magic wand that makes everything happen faster and better. Robots can build cars with incredible precision, and companies constantly improve your favourite apps and gadgets. The modern economy wouldn't be the same without these technological marvels. The job market is evolving too. Traditional jobs are shifting, and new ones are emerging. Careers like coding, data analysis, and digital marketing are in high demand, while some older roles are becoming less common. To thrive in this changing landscape, it's essential to keep learning and adapting. Lifelong learning is the name of the game.

In our quest to understand this world, we find that simplicity is our guiding star, leading us toward a more balanced and harmonious economic existence.

'Simplicity, simplicity, simplicity! I say, let your affairs be as one, two, three, and not a hundred or a thousand.'

Thoreau's exhortation resonates even more profoundly today when our lives are inundated with choices, ranging from smartphones to superfoods. Complexity has its place, but when it infiltrates every facet of our economic existence, we risk losing sight of the true essence of prosperity.

The modern global economy is marked by an incessant quest for growth. GDP numbers, stock market indices, and trade balances dominate our everyday discussions. As humans, we have lost the sight of the journey by being single-minded on the end goals. At this point, we need to remind ourselves constantly: Is this relentless pursuit of economic growth truly making us a happier species? As we toil away in the relentless pursuit of material wealth, are we not exchanging our precious time and energy for possessions that rarely bring lasting contentment?

We live in a world constantly bombarded by information and distractions, so it is easy to lose sight of what truly matters. Humans have become slaves to social media notifications, prisoners of our own desires, and oblivious to the broader economic and ecological consequences of our actions. Do we really need the newest gadget? How many times are we going to wear the new dress that was purchased on a whim? What about disposable plastic? Is it being recycled? Each transaction that we do has a ripple effect on the economy and the environment. It's time we harbour a more simplistic desire to reduce consumption and alleviate the stress on the environment.

It is true that a consumption-based economy goes hand-in-hand with innovation and development. And, it would be detrimental to stall the progress by reducing consumption just for the sake of it. The point to be noted here is not complete cessation of consumption, but a more moderated version of it. This would further development and the economy in a more sustainable manner. After all, we still don't have a Planet B to live on.

Herculean Labours to No End

In his book, *Walden*, Thoreau simplistically delineates every aspect of the economy that is misguided in principle. The challenges of the economy are essentially compared to the twelve labours of Hercules. However, the Herculean labours had a definite end to them. Each of them came with its own objective. The modern economy, however, is more like the Hydra slain by Hercules and Iolaus. Surmount one challenge, and we are presented with two more in its place. What's more, we don't have an Iolaus to pierce a hot iron rod to tackle the many-headed monster!

In today's world, we are basically handed everything on a silver platter. Everything is available at the touch of a button. Nobody has to strive hard to acquire anything. Who made technology the lieges and humans the serfs? Why is technology put on a pedestal while man is condemned to toil away at whacking through the weed of everyday challenges of the economy?

The majority of the populace does not till the soil or cleanse the proverbial Augean Stables. These people never had the luxury of having no encumbrances to live up to. But one thing is for sure. All of humankind labour under a mistaken assumption. Most of our labours in today's world amount for nothing. Once we die, the best parts of us are left to rot in the soil, or burnt up to a crisp ember. What about the challenges now? Does a dead soul think of the economy? The answer is a resounding 'No'.

Most humans meander ignorantly through the fields of life, preoccupied with superfluous desires and objective labours that they fail to pluck the sweet fruits of wisdom that life has got to offer. There is always something more than just economic growth and prosperity. One good long hard look at the poorest of the society will paint the true picture of the state of the economy.

Poor people eke out their daily living, gasping for breaths by the end of the day. They live on borrowed time, existing as if each day were to be the last. And yet, the so-called earning citizens of the modern economy are no different. Multitude of debts accrued through irrational spending makes us toil day after day to surmount the challenges that the Hydra of the modern economy throws at us.

We have become frivolous. We seek to curry favour. We live and die on borrowed money, promising to repay it as soon as we can. We rack up credit card debts. We take on mortgages that we can hardly afford to repay. We lie and flatter ourselves to project a nutshell of civility. Our very jobs that we depend on to sustain us sometimes reek of desperation. Then, when we age, we tender our resignation, to project ourselves to be further incapable. The younger generation lives in the desperate squalor that is games and amusements, despite not doing a hard day's work.

Sometimes, it appears as if we humans deliberately chose to perform these Herculean tasks that have no end to them, just for the sake of economic progress. We chose to project it as if there was no other alternative. But evidence based, and rational thinking states that it is never too late to abandon prejudices for the greater good. We must try to find ways to do things that consensus says cannot be done. We modern day humans have somehow irrationally managed to gloss out the accomplishments of our predecessors. They went through many ups and downs, and yet, we chose not to learn from their experiences while dealing with our day-to-day situations.

Thoreau aptly says, 'Humans trust a good deal more than their own actions.' And this is very true. We are presented a good deal for, say, a new laptop. Our minds have been so ingrained to think in a particular way to abandon the old and herald the new that we immediately jump at the proposition. We do not care about the e-waste that may arise during the disposal of the old laptop. We hardly care about the ecological damage that is caused while mining rare earths for the new laptop. All we care about is the waiving of the care of ourselves as we bestow our trust elsewhere.

So-Called Luxuries

Thoreau states that most of the luxuries, and most of the so-called comforts of life, have become so indispensable that they have turned hindrances to the elevation of mankind. Every individual has a different level of comfort that would satiate their desires. However, it is when we go overboard in doing things which ultimately lead us down the rabbit hole.

For example, a family of four would be more than comfortable in a three-bedroom house that is furnished with utilitarian items. There is one bedroom with a bed and wardrobe for the spouses and one bedroom each with a bed and wardrobe for each of the children. However, when the same family of four decides to move in to an eight-bedroom manor, replete with intricate furnishings and gold tasselled curtains; that is overdoing it; a palace that could house close to twenty people.

As humans, we have four main grand necessities in life viz. food, shelter, clothing, and income to support our sustenance. And yet, some of us become anxious and try to show-off that we have been blessed with more than what we need in any of the four aspects. We try to exaggerate the importance of the work we do by bragging about our salary with our peers. Yet, no one seems to understand that half of our work is actually not done by us. Technology does the majority while our minds do a miniscule of it.

For our shelters, we tend to overdo by decorating every nook and cranny of our humble abodes to make it as luxurious as possible. Did we ever stop to think that the wooden floor was cut from a mighty oak that was once home two hundreds of birds? Or did we stop to think about the chemical pollution that arises from the polymer-based decor in our houses? We drape ourselves in fur taken from poor unsuspecting animals. And finally, we also tend to gorge like gluttons on meat in portions that could feed a small army.

The success of scholars and philosophers lies in their humble courtier-like thoughts, and not kingly aspirations. Most of us are not kings, yet we want to live a life of one, thereby slipping into degeneracy. But why do we need to degenerate? Why should families run away from each other? What does luxury accord that elevates or destroys even nations?

All of us toil for the four grand necessities of life. Once acquired, instead of wanting a more opulent version, one must instead start indulging the smaller superfluities that life has to offer, such as going on a trek, taking up gardening, spreading acquired knowledge, etc. Man must root himself firmly onto the earth if he wants to soar above the heavens. Of course, people are of varied kinds, and there will inevitably be some of us who live life the way it ought to be lived. This is just a kind reminder to those of us who believe in the concept of so-called luxuries.

Strict Habits

For a more sustainable economy, new tradespersons must start cultivating better and stricter business habits. Let's delve into this with a small example. Imagine that you are an upcoming trader who wants to sell something to a neighbouring settlement on the other side of a vast river. Your assets must be an inventory warehouse and that's it. You must be the pilot of your own ship to transport the cargo. Your cargo must be products that your immediate environment produces, say, mangoes or timber for furniture. You must also be your own accountant to buy, sell, and keep accounts of all trades that happen.

This must go on until you have accrued enough capital to begin trading with distant shores, say another state in your country, or a different country altogether. At this juncture, more employees may be brought it depending on the size of the trade outposts that you wish to establish. Newer transportation methods could be used to transit cargo from your warehouses to the point of sales. Once a steady stream of income happens, it takes care of the grand necessity of income for sustenance.

With regards to the second grand necessity of clothing, the first and foremost concern should be whether the cloth that covers one's body retains vital heat and offers respite from external heat or cold. Anything else that the cloth does is purely cosmetic and an unwanted luxury. Kings and queens are used to wearing clothes that they would use but once. As everyday men, we need to choose clothes that have repeatability and tailored to fit. This builds one's character to the point that we would hesitate to buy unwanted clothes that do not suit our needs.

Shelter is the most important necessity of life after food. Every man, woman, and child must have a barebones shelter to keep them safe from the harsh elements of nature. Yet, there have been instances throughout history where people have been noted to survive without this basic need. The hardiest among us are the most satisfied with the rudimentary hutment, while the most unsatisfied among us are never content with even the most palatial of buildings. At the beginning of the human race, the primitive humans naturally yearned for some form of shelter. The first form of shelters were natural caves, which soon progressed to erecting settlements using leaves, branches, and bark of trees; all the way to the current sturdy wooden and concrete dwellings. If someone yearns to build a house in today's world, they needn't go back to the rudimentary form of living – that would be really inappropriate – but they can consider an abode that is more suited to their current lifestyle. Every human has the right to acquire and live in sheltered conditions. We need a comfortable house, built with sustainable materials that nature itself has to offer. Sure, there is the concept of rent, but isn't that more like paying a tax over the additional burden of so many existing taxation systems? On the other hand, building a shelter is no less cheap. In today's world, it costs more than half of an individual's lifetime earnings to build and maintain a house. That is really expensive. It is more like choosing between the lesser of the two evils.

However, building and owning a house is definitely considered to be a lesser of the evils since one cannot be evicted for failing to pay rent on time. Though one might question that paying a mortgage and paying rent are more or less the same, usually mortgages are tailored to fit an individual's income levels so that the person does not face financial difficulties. If an individual wants and gets a house beyond their means, he may not be richer but poorer for it, since it is the house that has obtained the human and not the other way round. Granted, the vast majority of people, especially in urban agglomerations, can afford to build or rent a modern house with all amenities. But what of the minority and the poor? The affordability of one class is neutralized by the wants of the other.

Most of us do not even realize the true meaning of a house/shelter over our heads. We trudge all our lives in building something that is the envy of our immediate neighbours in a needless show of one-upmanship. The closets are stacked with fur coats. Furniture is fit for a king and there are endless chambers for future guests who may or may not visit. A cellar is stocked with the most vintage of wines and the pantry is stocked with six months' worth of food. This has serious repercussions on the economy. This house is worth thrice our lifetime income. What happens if we fail to pay the mortgages on time? The house is repossessed; the bank is saddled with a non-performing asset, and thousands of such non-performing assets send the economy of a country into a tailspin, something that has already happened in our lifetime during the 2008 financial crisis.

An individual can indeed construct a house using lesser finances worth than a lifetime of paying rent for an equivalent house. Let's not confuse this with a boast. And if it does seem so, then humanity is indeed doomed to fail. Sacrifices need to be made at certain times, and building a lifelong shelter definitely calls for some sacrifices on our part. Hiring the right contractors with the right knowledge goes a long way in achieving the affordable house that we want. With regards to amenities, those are more like an illusion. Not all amenities advance us as a species. Sometimes, technology is overdone and over-reliance on the same can be detrimental. For example, a modern biometric lock and a manual locking system in a house do the same job. We mustn't let ourselves be distracted from the larger picture. The *Bhagavad Gita* aptly puts it, 'Towers and palaces are the luxury of princes, while a simple and independent mind doesn't toil to the bidding of any prince.'

The final grand necessity of life is food. Thoreau states in *Walden* that it is incredibly easy to obtain food for sustaining one's self. And in today's world, food is even easier to come by. We have never had so much surplus that we have today. Yet, we see daily stories of people living in malnutrition. The reason for that is unnecessary wastage. A simple diet that consists of meat, vegetables, cereals, and pulses is enough for a human to retain health. Salt has never been cheaper and drinking water has been provided to most of us. Yet, men have been known to starve, not for want of food, but for want of luxuries. Instead of water in a glass from a tap, people see the need to drink sparkling Perrier. Instead of locally grown and sourced meat and vegetables, people want to savour the finest meat or vegetables from far-off lands.

Readers, at this juncture, may perceive this as being spoken from an economic rather than dietary perspective. But they would be well served to know that our dietary habits often forge the economic engine. When one doesn't opt for locally sourced produce, it hits below the belt of a hardworking farmer. When one opts for drinking bottled water, it hits the government initiatives to provide safe drinking water to its people. All of earth's land is surrounded by abundant oceans that provide the necessary salt to season our food. Yet, people opt for chemically produced salt that comes in attractive packaging. While industries may thrive, people do not progress as a race. An economy can survive only if the lowest common denominator also progresses, in this case, the tradespersons of the community. We can even avoid the concept of trading and bartering for acquiring food by growing some of the produce ourselves, but as rightly put before, it hits below the belt of the honest farmer, hence the call for locally grown produce and meat.

Philanthropy

In the serene woods of Walden, Henry David Thoreau pondered the essence of life and our place in the world. As he observed the rhythms of nature and the simplicity of his own existence, he stumbled upon a profound insight: the power of philanthropy, the act of giving back to society. Thoreau's musings on this topic, though rooted in the nineteenth century, resonate just as strongly today. 'Philanthropy,' Thoreau wrote, 'is the gentle art of giving, a river of goodwill that flows through the human heart.'

In his rustic cabin by Walden Pond, he discovered that true wealth lay not in material possessions but in the riches of the soul, urging us to embrace the simple joy of giving.

The philosophy of philanthropy is not about grand gestures or enormous donations. Instead, it is about celebrating the everyday acts of kindness. Even the smallest acts of philanthropy, like helping a neighbour in need or planting a tree, can have a profound impact on the world. The reciprocal nature of philanthropy lies in the idea of 'in giving, we receive.' Walden's woods and waters, its flora and fauna, taught Thoreau the importance of harmony and balance, and he believed that society could learn from nature's wisdom. Thoreau stated that 'Philanthropy is the best way to restore balance to our human ecosystem.' Just as every species plays a vital role in the forest, every person has something to contribute to the greater good.

Thoreau was not blind to the challenges of his time, including poverty and inequality, something that exists even today. He believed that philanthropy was a remedy for these ills. 'We must not wait for governments to act. Each of us has a duty to make the world a better place.' Thoreau's call to action was a call to individual responsibility, a reminder that we are all stewards of our society. He found inspiration in self-reliance, a belief in one's own abilities. He saw philanthropy as an extension of this principle – a way for individuals to rely on their compassion and generosity to make a difference. He states that 'We have the power to shape our world, not through force, but through love.'

Thoreau's reverence for simplicity extended to his thoughts on philanthropy. He believed that giving should come from the heart, without expectation of recognition or reward. 'True philanthropy is anonymous,' he asserted. 'It is a silent force that hums beneath the surface, like the currents of Walden Pond.'

Even today, his wisdom remains relevant. In an age of complexity and noise, his call to simplicity in philanthropy reminds us that we can make a difference by embracing compassion and generosity.

As we navigate the challenges of the twenty-first century, we can draw inspiration from Thoreau's *Walden*. It is a reminder that philanthropy is not a distant concept reserved for the wealthy, but a timeless principle that each of us can practise in our own way. Thoreau's message is clear: in the quiet moments of our lives, in the depths of our hearts, we can find the power to make the world a better place through the gentle art of giving.

Chapter 7

The Government

The government should be a guardian of the people's aspirations, a custodian of justice, and a beacon of transparency, for in its actions, the true character of a society is revealed

Over the course of human history, there have been very few things that are as essential as the 'Government'. It is the invisible hand that guides our lives, the keeper of our collective aspirations, and the enabler of our shared progress. Whether you're a student in New York City, a farmer in rural India, or an entrepreneur in Lagos, the government plays an undeniable role in shaping the world around you. This exploration of the Government draws inspiration from Jean Jacques Rousseau's timeless work, *The Social Contract.* But in doing so, let's traverse the pages of history and reasonably understand it from a modern-day perspective. For that, we need to unravel the very essence of the government – what is it, why do we need it, and how does it affect our lives?

So what is the government? The government is like a grand conductor of a symphony, orchestrating the harmonious coexistence of diverse individuals within a society. It is the mechanism by which we collectively agree on rules, enforce order, protect our rights, and invest in the common good. A framework that holds the pieces of a puzzle together, allowing us to build our lives, careers, and communities within its boundaries. Governments come in various shapes and sizes – from democracies to monarchies, republics to autocracies. Each type has its own unique way of functioning, but at the heart of every government is the idea of serving the people.

Imagine a world without any government – a place where there are no rules, no justice system, and no one to protect your rights. It would be chaos and to mitigate this chaotic state, we need a government. The government acts as a social contract, an agreement between citizens and the state. In exchange for obeying the rules and paying taxes, the government provides security, infrastructure, education, and healthcare. It's the government that paves the roads you drive on, ensures the safety of your food, and defends your country from external threats. Without the government, there would be no order, no fairness, and no way to resolve disputes peacefully. In essence, the government exists to make our lives better, to create a society where we can thrive together.

Every day, the government impacts our life in ways one might not even notice. It sets the minimum wage, regulates the quality of the air we breathe, and decides the curriculum in our schools. The government also plays a crucial role in addressing social issues like poverty, inequality, and discrimination. It's the force behind policies that can either empower or hinder one's personal and professional growth. Moreover, governments shape the world order on a global scale. They engage in diplomacy, make international agreements, and tackle global challenges. The decisions made by our government can influence the fate of nations and the future of our planet.

In this grand social contract, citizens also bear responsibilities. We must participate in the democratic process, whether through voting or peaceful protest, to hold our government accountable.

We should strive to be informed, engaged, and active members of our communities. It's vital to remember that governments can make mistakes, and they can be swayed by special interests. It's our collective duty to speak up when we see injustice, to advocate for change, and to work towards a more just and equitable society.

The Political Body

An act of free will is said to possess two aspects to it: the first is the moral aspect which concerns with the determination to act in a certain manner, and the second is the physical aspect, which concerns the power to execute the determination. Imagine the following scenario. You are walking down a street and pass by a cake shop with a wonderful aroma emanating from it, making you yearn to have some cake. In order to buy the cake, your mind must want to go into the cake shop. And secondly, your feet must walk in the direction of the cake shop. A political body also works in a similar manner. The only difference lies in the terminologies we use to discern the forces.

In a political body, the physical force used to enact a law is considered as executive power while the very act of formulating laws to be enacted is called as legislative power. In the past chapters, we have seen that the power of legislation belongs to the people. The people of a society and their wants and wishes drive the political body to formulate a particular legislation. However, in case of the executive power, it solely lies with the government or the political body since it doesn't fall under the scope of any existing laws. In any case, the people of a society have enough free will to form a political body to repel the executive laws if they deem it to be detrimental.

So, what exactly constitutes a political body or the government? Is it the kings or magistrates or princes or governors or presidents? No. Those people merely exercise the rights of the political body; mere employees. A political body is one which conducts legitimate exercising of its executive powers and the head of the political body is one who discharges with the administrative duties of exercising the said executive powers in a legitimate manner. The head of the political body orders the executive branch of the government to formulate certain policies which are then presented to the people as such for consensus. This tripartite union stays in equilibrium if every participating member consents to the actions of the political body. However, the moment one of the members of the union, be it the head of state or the governing ministers or the subjects, does not consent, then a state of chaos prevails.

Imagine a country of a million people governed by a president whose sole job is to execute the powers of the government. Now, the president is related to the million people and each of the million people gets to own only a millionth part of the executive powers that the government has to offer. The more the number of people in the country, the more removed the individuals are from equality, since the share of the pie becomes miniscule.

In order to combat this, the political body devises division of the executive power via ministers, senators, governors; each with a constituent of people, so that individuals in those constituents have their fair share of equality when deciding to appoint a person to the executive level of the government. For example, ten thousand people out of the million would be responsible for electing a minister who would enact local laws for the people. The minister answers to the prime minister or president. Therefore, the share of the individual in the executive power comes to one in ten thousand rather than one in one million.

This continuous proportion of power between the political body, its administrators, and the people is not an arbitrary idea, but a necessary consequence of the nature of the political body itself. When people increase or decrease in number, or change harmonious existence through increased or decreased unity, the only ratio that changes is in terms of their relationship with the political body administrators and not the head itself. This shows that there is no concept of one size government fits all. Rather, it is a dynamic one. In order to clear any confusion, let us break the political body down to its brass tacks.

For a moment, let us assume that the administrators (governors, senators, ministers, councillors etc.) are a new body of the state, distinct from the head of the government and the people. The administrators are mere middlemen between the people and the head of the state. They simply enforce what is the will of the people (within legitimacy of existing laws) and nothing else. If in any situation the administrators enforce their own personal will either through force de jure or by de facto means, then it would mean the total dissolution of the political body itself, since it is no longer a harmonious tripartite union.

Although the work of the government is derived from the work of an ad hoc body, it still has a derivative and subordinate existence, according to Rousseau. He says that a political body can deviate from the norms as long as it doesn't digress from the objective for which the political body was created. He also says that the political body, which is best left to itself, tends to be the most corrupt. Hence, the political body needs a healthy relationship between the head of state, administrators, and the people.

Rousseau states that in a perfect system of a government, the action of individual wills accounts for nothing. However, in reality, four different wills constitute a political body/

government. The first will belongs to the individual. An individual's will is primarily concerned for its own well-being. The second will is the collective will of the administrators that do the work of the government. This can also be referred to as the corporate will. The third will is the collective will of the people as a whole. Though individuals may have their own wills, in a society, the will of the collective plays a major part in how a government acts and legislates. And lastly, the fourth will is that of the head of the state.

In a natural order, the will of the collective is said to be the weakest, the will of the sovereign the second, the will of the administrators the third, and the will of the individual being the strongest. This would then mean that individuals are themselves primarily, followed by being administrators, then the head of state, and lastly, a citizen; something that goes against the established societal norms where an individual is expected to be an honest citizen first. Now, what would happen if we elevated citizens to administrators, the administrators to the head of the political body, give utmost importance to individual will, and merge corporate will with that of the will of the individuals? In this case, the government will cease to act at full potential and will most certainly lead to anarchy and catastrophe.

The roles within a political body/government are definite and need not be changed. There is a reason why an administrator is so, because they perform the job better than common citizens. Similarly, a head of state is so, because that person has the supreme capacity to undertake the amalgamation of all the work done by the administrators. Sometimes, we must let prudence take over. It is fine to dream of being an administrator or a head of state, but one must also have the mental acuity to become one. Just like how too many cooks spoil the broth, too many individual wills in the running of a state are most likely to lead to the collapse of society.

Different Types of Government

By now, it is indelible that a government consists of many moving parts. But the government itself has different forms. A government can be classified based on how it functions and the members that constitute a government. In this section, we shall see in detail on how different forms of government are demarcated for classification.

Governments come in a variety of forms, each characterized by distinct principles and structures. Democracy, for instance, is a system where power resides with the people, and citizens elect their leaders through free and fair elections. The central principle of democracy is 'popular sovereignty,' emphasizing that ultimate authority rests with the collective will of the people. In this system, the general will plays a pivotal role in shaping laws and policies, reflecting the interests and desires of the citizenry. On the other hand, monarchy represents a different form of governance, where supreme authority is vested in a single individual, often a king or queen. This system operates on the principle of 'hereditary rule,' meaning that leadership is inherited within a royal family. Monarchies can take various forms, ranging from absolute monarchies, where the monarch holds extensive power, to constitutional monarchies, where the monarch's authority is constrained by a constitution or elected representatives.

In a republic, elected representatives take on the responsibility of making decisions on behalf of the people. The key principle underlying a republic is 'representative democracy'. Citizens exercise their democratic rights by electing officials who act as their representatives in crafting laws and policies. Republics can encompass a range of governance structures, including parliamentary and presidential systems.

In contrast to these more inclusive forms of government, authoritarianism places power in the hands of a single leader or a small group. Decision-making in authoritarian governments is centralized. Individual freedoms and political opposition are often curtailed in favour of maintaining tight control over the state. Totalitarianism takes authoritarianism to an extreme, where the government exercises absolute control over every facet of citizens' lives, from politics and the economy to culture and social norms. The core principle here is 'total authority', with the state employing tools such as propaganda, censorship, and surveillance to maintain an iron grip on society.

Federalism, on the other hand, represents a different approach to governance, dividing power between a central authority and smaller regional entities. This system is guided by the principle of 'shared sovereignty,' ensuring that both the central government and regional governments possess distinct powers and responsibilities.

Theocracy is yet another form of government where religious leaders or religious texts hold sway over political decisions and policies. Theocracy is rooted in the principle of 'divine rule', whereby religious authority guides political governance, often entwining specific religious beliefs and institutions with the state. History is peppered with accounts of states being ruled by religious leaders, such as the Islamic Caliphate by the Saracens, Christian kingdoms in the Middle East and Europe, and more recently, the Islamic republics in the Middle East.

These diverse forms of government each have their own strengths, weaknesses, and implications, reflecting the unique values and priorities of the societies in which they are implemented.

Democracy

An old saying goes thus – 'He who makes the laws, knows best how to enact and enforce it.' Therefore, the best form of government would be where executive power is united with the legislative power. However, it is this very argument what makes a government woefully inadequate. Nothing can be more dangerous than the influence of private will on public affairs. When a government bends existing laws, it is still a lesser evil compared to that of a corrupt head of state enforcing their personal will. Consequently, a government that doesn't abuse the independence of its people would always be in charge of the people due to good governance. Good governance of people would lead to people not needing governance at all.

Sadly, democracy has never existed, and most likely never will, in its truest and strictest definition. The very idea of democracy goes against the will of the natural order of majority should govern and the minorities should be governed. It is impossible to assume that people would partake in governmental affairs on a daily basis. In a true democracy, localized power is vested in the hands of administrators to ensure the best for their constituents.

'Democracy is not merely a system of governance; it's the embodiment of the people's voice, the canvas where diverse ideas paint the portrait of progress, and the compass guiding nations toward a brighter future.' As evidenced by this statement, democracy is the best way to ensure that the voices of the people, even in the lowest strata of the society, are heard loud. Without the form of government that democracy has to offer, the voices of these people would most likely be suppressed and these people would be left to rot on the so-called path to progress. Democracy offers the people to exercise their dissent without the fear of repercussions. If there is dissatisfaction with administrators, democracy offers people the chance to usher in newer faces for the post.

The formation of a democratic system of governance is not an easy matter. First off, the political body must be willing to decentralize power by appointing the posts of administrators. Then, people must be willing to coalesce as a group to acknowledge the presence of these administrators and elect suitable persons for those posts. This requires consensus, something that is hard to arrive at. However, democracy caters to the rule of the majority, so if the majority of the people reach consensus on appointing a particular administrator, then it is done. Next, the coalesced people must be willing to partake in discussing thorny issues that have plagued their society. Lastly, the administrators must enact laws that have as little luxury attached to it as possible. Rousseau states that luxury corrupts the poor and the rich equally in a society. The rich own too many assets for their own good, while the poor begin to covet these riches. This would ultimately transform the country into a vain one and not a democratic one.

Like all governments, democracy would also be subjected to internal strife and civil wars; perhaps more so than the other forms due to the prevailing law of the people. As such, the democratic government tends to be a more dynamic one, always listening to its people. In a democratic government, every citizen is beholden to remain steadfast and courageous to shape their own way in a system that offers them plenty of opportunity to do so.

Finally, there is a Latin saying by Palatine – '*Malo periculosam libertatem quam quietum servitium*' meaning 'liberty fraught with danger is more acceptable than peace under servitude'. Sure, democracy is fraught with perils at every step of the way, and in fact, many things need to work in harmony for the system to work perfectly. However, the liberty which a democratic system offers is unrivalled to the other systems of the government.

Aristocracy and Monarchy

When societies initially formed, it was more or less governed by the most powerful families living within that society. The heads of those families deliberated among themselves about various public affairs while the younger members of the society readily submitted to the wisdom of the elders. But as societies grew and matured, people started associating power with wealth. Transfer of riches and power happened between father to children, thereby creating a patrician society and governmental affairs hereditary. This led to extraordinary circumstances where heads of state were as young as six or seven years old, like Tutankhamen in Egypt.

Aristocracy can be of three forms – natural, elective, and hereditary. Of these, elective aristocracy is said to be the best form and true to the definition of aristocracy, where people can choose to elect their leaders on their perception of power. Hereditary aristocracy is the worst, where people may be ruled by absolute despots just because they hold the most power. Nevertheless, an aristocracy is often considered the most natural way of governance, where the wisest of the society rules over others. An aristocracy requires lesser virtues to govern, but also comes with its own set of peculiarities to begin with.

It requires moderating the rich and ensuring contentment among the poor. This calls for equality on a scale that has never before seen in history, even among the great aristocracies of ancient Greece. The administrative aspects of governance must always be entrusted to those who can devote undivided attention to the same. By this definition, rich people have the most undivided time to spare, but a poor and wise man may have equally undivided attention for matters of governance.

In a monarchy, the power of governance is concentrated in the hands of a natural born leader, who alone is considered to have the right to use his or her power according to established laws. This person is called a monarch. If the monarch is a male, then they are referred to as a king, while the female monarch is referred to as the queen. In monarchy, a single individual represents the will of the collective. The moral unity of the collective is also equated to the physical will of the collective and the monarch. The administrators, monarch, and the subjects, all obey the same power centre, which is the monarch. The system offers no counteractions to the state machinery.

Monarchs often wish to become absolute centres of power, so they do everything to hold on to their power base. The first order of things is to gain the respect and love of their subjects. However, Rousseau states that gaining the love of people is conditional, since individuals by themselves are quite fickle. All it takes is a strong-minded individual in the society to tell the other members that they would be better off living as a collective rather than being lorded upon by an individual who wishes nothing more than to be a master. Most successful monarchs keep their subjects weak-minded so that there is no resistance to the monarch.

In general, monarchy is more suited to large states with divisions of power occurring amongst princes, nobles, earls, counts, etc. All of the lower-level royals answer to the supreme monarch and the subjects answer to these lower-level royals. This way, the ratio of the people to the supreme monarch is not diluted, and people still have a say in what the lower-level royals do. However, the public voice hardly rises above the lower royals and, in most cases, does not reach the supreme monarch.

Most of the successful courtiers in monarchies are weasels and people with petty talents that satisfy the whims of the monarch rather than the people. This is one major drawback which stunts the monarchy. Then the problem of succession arises. What happens when the monarch dies without an heir? Will the kingdom be divided equally amongst the lower royals? Or will the state be subject to ceaseless strife in a quest for power? Sure, the crown has been made hereditary in most kingdoms, but regencies are always under the threat of power usury.

Mixed Governments

If the annals of history are anything to go by, there is no such thing as a perfect form of government. A monarch must always have subordinates and a democratically elected head of state must always rely on administrators for good governance. In a good governing system, there exists a grading of power from the majority to the minority, which will ensure that the political body always works for the betterment of the society.

However, sometimes, mixed governments may just be the answer to the solution. The states of England, Sweden, and the Netherlands are prime examples. The monarch is the head of state in these countries, while the affairs of the political body, such as administration and legislation, are left to a council of ministers. It needs to be noted that this system can work only if there is a mutualistic dependency between the monarchy and the council of ministers. If there is an equal bifurcation of power, then cohesion is lost and the country is the one that shall suffer.

Let us look at how a mixed government functions with the help of a mixed stew as an example. In a mixed stew, there are various ingredients that are combined to make the perfect dish. Just like that, a mixed government blends the strength of various systems to create a system of governance that orchestrates stability, liberty, and justice in a flavourful unity. Nevertheless, this may not be suited for all countries or states, since the state is essentially a product of the will of the collective living within it.

Dictatorship and Censorship

It is never a good idea to establish obdurate centres of power that suspend laws and pay no heed to consequences of the same. History has borne witness to some of the ancient kingdoms like Sparta doing the very same, which historians theorize may have been one of the underlying causes of the fall of the Greek Empire. Public order must never be interfered with unless the fate of the country hangs in the balance. In this case, it is acceptable to concentrate the executive powers in the hands of a few or even one, but never at other times.

The Romans were very famous in adopting the term dictator for the supreme leader of the Senate of the Roman Empire. So why were they called dictators in the first place? Rome was initially established as a Republic, which gradually transformed into an empire. The empire needed a special Consul, which the senate appointed via vote. The Consul came to be known as *dicere,* meaning one who spoke during the times of emergency and the rise of the Roman Empire was considered an emergency in the Roman Republic.

In contemporary usage, a dictator typically refers to a ruler with absolute and often oppressive power over a country, whereas in ancient Rome, the dictator was a temporary and exceptional office intended to restore order during crises. In modern parlance, dictatorship is the everlasting darkness that arises when the flame of liberty is extinguished. It is a reminder of enduring human desire for free will. While they may promise stability and efficiency, dictatorships are often associated with a lack of political freedoms, censorship, and the suppression of dissent. The history of dictatorships is marked by both periods of stability and prosperity, as well as instances of tyranny and oppression, making them a subject of complex analysis in the realm of political science and global affairs.

In the realm of political philosophy, one finds a rich vein of thoughts and discourses on the concept of censorship, a subject that has long captivated the minds of thinkers and leaders alike. Through Rousseau's lens, we can examine the delicate balance between the preservation of order and the protection of individual freedoms, and how censorship often becomes a contentious point in this philosophical dialogue. Rousseau's central premise in *The Social Contract* is the idea of the general will, which represents the collective will of the people as a whole. He argues that in a just society, individuals come together to form a social contract, willingly surrendering some of their individual liberties for the common good. The general will, as he articulates, should reflect the common interests and desires of the citizenry.

One might wonder how censorship intersects with Rousseau's notion of the general will. Rousseau, in his writings, did not explicitly endorse or condemn censorship, but his ideas can shed light on the subject. Censorship, when applied judiciously, can be seen as a tool to safeguard the general will and maintain social harmony and protect the collective interests of the community. However, the very concept of censorship also raises concerns about the potential infringement upon individual freedoms. Rousseau emphasized the importance of individual liberty and the need for citizens to participate in the creation of laws that reflect the general will. Censorship, when overstepped, can infringe upon the rights of individuals to express themselves freely.

Rousseau states that censorship should be guided by the principles of preserving the general will while respecting the fundamental rights of individuals. This requires utmost discernment and caution during the implementation of censorship measures. Rousseau's philosophy also emphasizes the role of government in maintaining this equilibrium. When censorship is employed, it should be within the framework of laws created through a democratic process that genuinely reflects the general will of the people. Rousseau's philosophy also offers a warning against the perils of excessive censorship. He argues that when censorship goes beyond the preservation of social order and the common good; it risks eroding the very foundations of a just society. Unchecked censorship can lead to the domination of a ruling elite or the suppression of dissenting voices.

The Signs of a Good Government

What makes a government good? Unfortunately, this question doesn't have an acceptable answer from any perspective, since the matter is purely subjective. What is done by the government may be good in the eyes of one group of citizens, but despicable in the eyes of another. However, when one asks about the signs of good or bad governance over people, this can, in fact, be determined.

Though this too is not a settled matter since everyone decides in their own way what is good and bad, it can be answered better than the former question. In authoritarian, monarchical, and aristocratic governments, the subjects extol tranquility. So, to these people, these types of governments would be a sign of good governance. However, in democratic governments, citizens value individual freedoms. To them, any government that promotes public discourse is a good government.

It is often said that morality cannot be precisely measured. So even if consensus exists on the signs of good governance, how do we go about evaluating them? Rousseau, in *The Social Contract*, says there is one simple method for overcoming this problem. The main objective of a political body is to ensure the security and prosperity of its members. The surest sign that they are safe and prospering is the growth in population. Without any other factor in consideration like external funding, immigrant naturalization, external territories, etc., the government under which a population boom is recorded can be stated to be a sign of a good government. This is because the government has presented a set of factors to its population that are conducive for growth and prosperity without the fear of regressing. Conversely, a government under which the people decay and population decreases is the worst government.

From a modern-day context, the signs of a good government are not limited to just population increase alone. There are many other factors to be considered. In a well-functioning government, the rule of law is paramount. This means that laws are applied consistently and impartially to all citizens, including those in positions of power. A good government holds its officials accountable for their actions, ensuring that no one is above the law. Transparency and mechanisms for addressing corruption and abuses of power are essential aspects of accountability. A strong government respects and protects the individual rights and freedoms of its citizens. Citizens should feel secure in the knowledge that their rights are upheld and protected by the government.

Good governance entails the efficient provision of essential services such as healthcare, education, infrastructure, and public safety; a government that can effectively manage resources and deliver services to its citizens. Next, a government that encourages citizen participation and representation is more likely to be considered good. Elected officials should genuinely represent the diverse interests of the population, fostering a sense of inclusivity and democracy. Another modern-day sign of a good government includes policies that promote job creation, equitable distribution of wealth, and sustainable economic growth. Effective economic management and fiscal responsibility are hallmarks of good governance.

In today's world, social justice is an equally important factor in determining a good government. It must implement policies that ensure equal access to opportunities, resources, and benefits for all citizens, regardless of their background or socioeconomic status. A good government also respects the inherent dignity of all individuals and acknowledges the importance of cultural diversity within its borders. It fosters an environment where different cultures can coexist harmoniously.

Effective governance includes long-term planning and vision for the future. A government that considers the well-being of future generations and takes measures to protect the environment and resources demonstrates foresight and responsibility. A government should be responsive to the evolving needs and concerns of its citizens. This involves listening to feedback, addressing grievances, and adapting policies to reflect changing circumstances and priorities. Finally, ensuring the safety and security of its citizens is a fundamental duty of any government. A good government works to maintain internal stability, resolve conflicts peacefully, and protect its nation from external threats.

Chapter 8

The Free Spirit

The Free Spirit soars above the clouds of conformity, finding liberation in the boundless sky of self-discovery .

Till now, we have seen the origin of societies, survival of the fittest, forming social contracts, states, leaders, economies, and the government itself. But it is time we took a good look within ourselves. None of the above is possible without the presence of an individual. And an individual is born with free will and free spirit. Friedrich Nietzsche, the enigmatic nineteenth-century German philosopher, stood as a sentinel of intellectual rebellion in an age marked by societal conformity and stifling moral conventions. His philosophy challenged the very foundations of established thought, urging individuals to break free from the chains of tradition and embrace the concept of the free spirit.

Nietzsche's intellectual journey was a radical departure from the prevailing philosophical currents of his time. While the nineteenth century was marked by a resurgence of traditionalism and moral absolutism, Nietzsche offered a radical counter-narrative. He questioned the validity of established morality, asserting that it was often a tool of repression and conformity. Nietzsche saw the free spirit as the embodiment of a courageous and independent thinker unburdened by the weight of conventional morality. The free spirit, as envisioned by him, represents an individual who dares to interrogate the moral codes and values that society imposes. Nietzsche argued that the free spirit is unafraid to challenge conventional wisdom, even if it means traversing uncharted intellectual territory. In this quest for personal autonomy, the free spirit finds liberation.

One of Nietzsche's central tenets was the idea of the 'will to power'. He believed that every individual possesses an innate drive to assert their own unique will and exercise their autonomy. The free spirit, guided by this inner compulsion, strives to transcend societal norms and restrictions. He saw this as a vital aspect of human flourishing. The free spirit, however, is not merely a rebel without a cause. Nietzsche did not advocate for a nihilistic rejection of all moral values. Instead, he called for the creation of new values, ones that emerge from the individual's authentic experience and self-expression. In this sense, the free spirit is not a destroyer of meaning but a creator of meaning.

To Nietzsche, the free spirit embodies the spirit of authenticity. It is an invitation to live a life that is true to oneself, untainted by the prejudices and expectations of others. The free spirit does not conform to external standards of success or happiness, but seeks to define their own path to fulfilment. In embracing authenticity, individuals become the authors of their own narratives, crafting a life that resonates with their innermost desires and aspirations. Nietzsche's vision of the free spirit has far-reaching implications for society as a whole. It challenges us to reevaluate our preconceived notions of right and wrong, urging us to scrutinize the moral codes that have been handed down. In doing so, it opens the door to a more inclusive and pluralistic understanding of morality.

Furthermore, the concept of the free spirit has profound implications for creativity and innovation. In a world where conformity often stifles originality, the free spirit serves as a beacon of inspiration. It encourages us to think beyond the confines of established norms and to cultivate a culture that values innovation, experimentation, and the pursuit of novel ideas. Nietzsche's philosophy of the free spirit also invites us to confront the discomfort of uncertainty and ambiguity. Embracing the unknown and venturing into uncharted territory can be a daunting prospect. However, it is precisely in these moments of uncertainty that the free spirit finds its greatest opportunities for growth and self-discovery. It is a call to embrace the chaos of existence with open arms and to find meaning in the process of becoming.

Simplification

The wonders of simplicity are quite amazing! It's quite strange how we humans live our lives by just simplifying and sometimes even distorting things. It's remarkable when you start noticing this. We've made everything around us so clear and straightforward that we are unable to perceive the unknown. We've moulded our senses to easily understand the surface of things that sometimes, our thoughts prefer playful tricks and incorrect conclusions rather than looking at things the right way. From the start, we've managed to keep ourselves in the dark about certain things so that we can enjoy a sense of freedom, carelessness, recklessness, and cheerfulness that's almost beyond belief.

Our ability to remain ignorant about certain things has provided a sturdy foundation for knowledge to grow. Knowledge has thrived on the solid rock of ignorance. This might sound strange, but the desire for knowledge has been built on top of a much stronger desire for ignorance, uncertainty, and even things that aren't true. We can therefore say that knowledge is not the opposite of ignorance; in fact, it's a more refined form of it. We hope that language, not just here, but in general, continues to stumble when trying to describe opposites where there are only varying degrees and subtle differences. We also hope that the moral hypocrisy that's deeply ingrained in our nature won't succeed in twisting the words in the mouths of those who can see through it. Every now and then, we understand this hypocrisy and find it amusing how even the best knowledge tries to keep us in a simplified, artificially constructed, carefully imagined, and somewhat distorted world. Knowledge loves life, and errors are a part of life.

Now that the mirth is out of the way, let us get serious. One must take great care when doing or saying something for 'truth's sake', for it sullies the innocence and neutrality of one's conscience. It can make you stubborn in the face of criticism and opposition. It can make you dull, less human, and even savage when you have to face danger, slander, suspicion, expulsion, or worse because you're defending the truth. In reality, 'The Truth' is not as weak and helpless as one makes it to be. It doesn't need defenders like us or the thinkers. 'The Truth' speaks for itself.

It doesn't really matter if we win or lose arguments. Philosophers of their day hardly made their cases. It is in retrospect that they have been lauded as great minds of their time. Sometimes, all it takes is a simple question mark at the end of words and sentences. It is more powerful than arguing in the court of law to defend against accusers. Sometimes, it is better to hide and avoid the fight altogether. We need to keep ourselves sane in the craziness of today's world, and for that, we need to surround ourselves with people who are like soothing music we can listen to while soaking in a hot tub at the end of a long, long day.

We all need peace to live our lives the way we want to. But total solitude is never the answer. Underhanded conflicts sans the use of force are not good for us in the long run, for it makes us testy and crafty individuals. It leads to paranoia thinking that every single person is an enemy or could be one. The outcasts of the society, persecuted people, and even ones that choose to be alone can turn into vindictive people seeking revenge. Sacrifice for the sake of truth forces even the most artistic minded people to become rebels of the society. Not only leading to moral depredation, but also to the degradation of the very fabric of society itself.

To be fair, developing darker shades to one's moral character is not a bad thing in itself. But it must not come at the cost of one's true objectives. Not every philosophical thought has its origins in a tragic story and every philosopher is not a martyr, but an individual who has had their moral compass reset.

Privacy

Every person, be it an extraordinary genius or the everyday common man, is prone to seeking a place they can call their own. It's their fortress of solitude if you want to relate to pop culture fiction. This fortress of solitude is a personal space where one can be free from the crowd, the masses, and the common ways of the world. It's a place where one can escape from being like everyone else and instead be exceptional. The only exception to this is when commoners are irresistibly drawn to those who are even more exceptional. It is perfectly fine to feel a bit out of place from time to time when it comes to dealing with others. It is perfectly fine to feel fed up, feel bored, feel sympathetic, gloomy, and many more emotions. It is only considered abnormal when a person doesn't feel these things. Now, it may seem harsh to call those unfeeling people as dilettantes but for want of a better word, let's stick to it.

Conversely, if a person actively avoids these feelings and prefers to stay hidden away, then it's pretty clear: they're not meant to attain greater knowledge. Because to truly know things, one has to be willing to deal with all these ups and downs, including the not-so-pleasant experiences. Gaining knowledge is not all about seeking privacy and thinking profound thoughts. On the contrary, it involves a lot of studying the mannerisms of people around us. No matter how uncomfortable we may feel, sometimes it involves putting on an act and hanging around with people we may not desire to be around. However, this also leads to finding like-minded people who can make life's journey seem so much more comfortable. Society has a very derogatory term for like-minded people and refers to them as cynics, but cynicism is about as much honesty a person can give you without being saint-like.

In order to gain more knowledge, one must shun unwanted privacy and be open to more of cynicism (both rough and refined versions of it). Though cynicism can come off as being vile, it also has a fascinating outlook about it. Cynics are dirty. There's no easier way to put it. But they are also incredibly sharp-witted and profound in their thinking; much more than the so-called intellects who are conformists. More often than not, a brilliant mind is stuck with a less than radiant personality. Psychologists are the best example for them. But do they actively seek out privacy? No. Their entire job is to study people and their behaviours.

Only by interacting with people can we know more about ourselves, like our needs for food, sex, and emotional contact. We tend to know more about what drives us when we interact with people. So it behoves us to pay attention to what people around us are talking about. Unwanted privacy can lead to a manifestation of unwanted anger. This consequently leads to us tearing things apart – be it ourselves, God, or the society around us. We may come off as morally superior when we have a sense of aloofness about us, but this only makes us seem banal and less knowledgeable. And anyone who indignantly says otherwise is the biggest liar of us all.

Language

By now, we have established that to gain knowledge, an individual must shun unwanted privacy and interact with others. This brings us to a unique challenge, the language barrier. One of the most challenging things in life is to translate from one language to another, while maintaining its unique rhythm and pace of its style. The pace of a language is rooted in the character of the people who speak it. In a more 'simplistic' way, it refers to the average speed at which people of a particular culture perceive and imbibe certain ideologies. Sometimes, even with the best intentions, translations can unintentionally simplify or even distort the original text. This happens because the lively and cheerful tempo of the original can be difficult to capture while translating it.

For instance, the German language often struggles with achieving a quick and lively pace in writing. This means that many of the most delightful and bold nuances of free and spirited thought can be challenging for Germans to express. German literature has a tendency to become heavy, dense, and pompously complicated, sometime bordering on the verbose. Prose of various German writers, for example Goethe and Nietzsche himself, has a unique blend of rigidity and prosaic elegance. This is mainly reflective of the time at which the texts were written, often conforming to existing rules and customs. Nietzsche's work *Beyond Good and Evil* kind of broke the conformist style by introducing elements of humour in it. However, this apparent lack of humour in the German writing style often meant that they could not understand the silliness of clown humour or even political satire.

Forget the Germans; even native English speakers cannot understand the tempo at which Machiavelli takes the readers to the dry, fresh air of Florence in 'The Prince.' In that work, serious ideas are often presented with an impish style. It is kind of oxymoronic since the way in which Machiavelli presents his ideas are in direct contrast to the dangerous concepts he discusses. This is something English can never hope to achieve. Then, there was Plato in Ancient Greece; a man who despised every flaw that Ancient Greece had to offer. Yet, he was fond of the witty writings of Aristophanes, the tempo of something that cannot be replicated in any other language except for Greek.

Language barriers can be both a challenge and an opportunity on the path to attaining a free spirit and acquiring knowledge. Learning new languages is a powerful way to break down these barriers and can help establish connections with people from different cultures. In addition to language learning, modern technology provides valuable tools like translation apps, which aid communication across language barriers. These tools, while not perfect, can facilitate basic conversations and help in understanding foreign languages. Active listening is also a crucial skill when dealing with language barriers. One must learn to pay attention to tone, intonation, and context in conversations, as they provide valuable clues about the speaker's emotions and intentions, even if you don't grasp every word. This skill fosters empathy and cultural understanding.

While facing language barriers, it's essential to remain patient and humble. Misunderstandings and mistakes may occur, but embracing the learning process and being open to correction are essential. Building a support network is valuable in navigating language barriers. Language exchange partners, language tutors, and local friends can assist with translation, language learning, and offering insights into their culture. Seeking common ground with others can transcend language barriers. Shared interests, hobbies, or experiences provide a foundation for communication and connection, regardless of language. Activities like sports, music, art, or cooking often serve as universal languages that bring people together.

Origins of Actions

For most of human history, especially in what we call the prehistoric times, people judged whether an action was good or bad based on its outcomes, not on the action itself or where it came from. Just like today's world, where a child's actions are reflective of parenting methods, success or failure of outcomes influenced how people viewed an action. Nietzsche refers to this period as the 'pre-moral' period because the concept of 'know yourself!' didn't exist yet among humans. But in the last ten thousand years or so, especially in some parts of the world, things changed. Whether it was for the better or not is debatable, but instead of focusing on the consequences of an action, people started caring more about the origins of an action i.e. why to act in a particular manner. This was a big step forward for humankind. It happened because of aristocratic values and the belief in 'origin'. Nietzsche referred to this period as the 'moral era', and it marked the first attempt at understanding ourselves. A paradigm shift in perspective occurred, where instead of looking at the effects of an action, we looked at its starting point.

However, this change also brought about a new belief. People began to think that the value of an action depended entirely on its intention, basically what someone meant to do instead of why they did it. Society in general began to believe that an action's worth was determined by its intention.

But in today's world, there might be a need to rethink this idea. Philosophers like Nietzsche have long theorized that we've reached a point in life where a radical rethought of our value system is needed in order to avoid slipping into an 'ultra-moral' period. This is to avoid being viewed as immoral. Nietzsche says, in *Beyond Good and Evil,* that immoral thinkers suspect that the true worth of an action lies much deeper than what is intentional.

The intention to act is just a sign that the act itself needs further explanation. This can be interpreted in many ways, so rendering it meaningless. However, that is not always true. The act of a mother feeding her child needs no further explanation. It is innate and natural. However, the act of bombing a children's hospital in the garb of religious vendetta is unnatural, and the act needs further interpretation. It can quickly be attributed to misguided morals but equating morality to intentions would create a biased outlook that can be proven wrong. From Nietzsche's writings, it is clear that we need to move past the concept of morality while judging the origins and intentions behind an individual's actions. The journey of overcoming or redefining morality is a task for the most refined, upright, and even the most wicked of consciences of today, as they challenge and reshape our understanding of the human soul.

Moral Naiveté

No matter one's origins, cultural upbringing, morality, or type of government in their country, it is impossible to deny that the world we live in is error prone. We have been inculcated to think and act in a certain manner, and yet, upon rational thought, we find something or someone has been deceiving us all along. It is very easy to blame rational thinking for perceiving world as an error infested place and the lies it unearths. Lest we forget, rational thinking is that taught us that the earth moved around the sun and not the other way around. Rational thinking gave us the concept of gravity and time.

But if someone believes things to be otherwise, they might start to doubt thinking itself. That is why history is littered with stories of conspiracy theorists who believed that the moon landings were faked, Hitler is still alive, and the Great Pyramid of Giza was built by an alien civilization. But is it wrong to say that rational thinking hasn't tricked us before? Thinkers unfettered by morality have a kind of innocence that's admirable. They still retain the naiveté to ask questions like whether the world is 'real' and why it seems to keep its true nature hidden. Philosophers tend to believe in immediate certainties due to their simplistic morality. But in today's world, we need to be more than just moral thinkers. It would be utter foolishness to base our thought process on moral thinking. Society thinks that curiosity bordering on suspicion is a sign of bad character growth. But to truly grow in life, we need to break free of the shackles of these middle-class norms. A bit of imprudence is not bad, as long as we don't make a fool of ourselves in the process. A bit of suspicion is good to question things since people have been fooled since times immemorial.

Sure, the concept would seem dreary and gloomy but do not be put off. Deception and being deceived are two different entities. The former is a result of unscrupulous morals and the latter is a result of moral naiveté. It is time we learn to differentiate the two. Truth is much more than moral assumptions and appearances. Our free spirit must not be hindered by the worst-supported ideas of morality governing actions and consequences. Though life itself relies on how we perceive things around us, we must learn to delineate the boundaries that separate the 'seeming' from the truth. So, is there a mountain of difference between what is true and what is false? What would happen if we assume that the world we live in is a simulation? Doesn't every simulation need a creator? What if the creator of our simulation is the Supreme Entity that is revered as God by the multitude of cultures around the world? We can answer it by asking a counter question. Why does a creator need to exist? If everything is fictional, why can't everything arise spontaneously? In English, grammar and usage is played around to make more emphatic statements. Perhaps it is time we applied the same to our everyday lives.

Logic

Imagine for a moment that the only real thing in this world is our own desires and passions. We are forbidden to think of anything except for our impulses. However, what is thinking? Isn't it a byproduct of how these impulses relate to each other? We can try to correlate the mechanical and material aspects of this world to our emotions and desires. But will it work? Will it have the same level of reality as what we experience through our emotions? Maybe it's like an earlier version of our emotional world, where everything is connected in a strong unity before it separates into different processes in our bodies, like digestion, breathing, and growth. Can we see it as a basic form of life where all these functions are still closely connected? Can we think of it as the primal way of life?

In the end, logical thinking dictates that this is the right way to approach this question. We shouldn't assume different types of causality like how one set of things cause other things unless we've thoroughly explored the idea of having just one type of causality. In today's world, this is a methodological rule we just can't afford to ignore. It's a part of the logical reasoning process. The main question is whether logical thinking would allow us to truly believe in the will as something that causes things to happen and whether we believe in the causality of the will. If logical thinking permits us to do so, while retaining the core tenet that our beliefs and causality are the same, then as individuals we must try to imagine that the will is the only causality. Using this, we can see that logical thinking will tell us that the 'will' can only affect other 'wills,' and not physical things like nerves or matter. Going back to the concept of origins of actions, an individual's actions and subsequent effects can be logically inferred to be a result of the willpower behind it.

Now, let's say we manage to tie in the instinctive actions to willpower. Suppose we can trace all bodily functions to this willpower, including how life is created and how our body sustains itself for nourishment. Logically speaking, we can then define all forms of life force as willpower. The entire world and its workings could simply be defined as acts of willpower.

Truth

In today's world, most people don't automatically accept a belief as being true just because it makes them happy or virtuous. Our minds have been conditioned over the years to question everything and get to the bottom of the barrel to seek the correct answers. Nietzsche says that the only exception to this rule might be the kind-hearted 'Idealists' who are passionate about good and basal things like truth and beauty. Idealists tend to mix various desires, both good and not-so-good, in their thinking, which leads them to think in the extremes. If something they believe in makes them happy, then the belief must be true. If something what they believe in makes them unhappy, then the belief must be wrong.

Happiness and virtue alone aren't enough to prove something is true, especially in current times when people are overloaded with information via the internet and social media. However, we also conveniently overlook the fact that unhappy people or promoting vile things, or spewing hate on social media platforms isn't evidence contrary to the truth either. Certain facts could be true even if they go against our line of thought. For example, we may believe that silk has been obtained through peaceful means, while reality is that the cocoons of the silkworm are dipped in boiling water to kill the worms and to extract the silk thread from the cocoon itself. It is a happy coincidence that we humans forgo some of the truth in order to stay sane. In fact, organizing life in this way is for the best, since knowing too much truth could simply overwhelm us.

Society judges the mental strength of an individual by how much truth a person can handle. Not only the quantity, society also perceives the mental aptitude of an individual by how they can palate the truth when it is presented on a silver platter, easy to bear, or when it is disguised in many forms.

However, it's clear that some wicked people or the more unfortunate ones have the unwanted privilege of discovering certain aspects of truth that are not easily perceived by the commoners of the public. Wicked people, especially wicked happy people, are a group of moralists who don't discuss much about the truth itself. They are often tough and cunning, which may present them with better chances of getting to the bitter truth or even the more distorted ones. And it is no coincidence that strong and independent thinkers are usually shrewd and get to the truth, while the gentler lot often beat around the bush while trying to arrive at the truth. Of course, this assumes that we don't restrict the label 'philosopher' to those who write books or explicitly talk about their philosophy.

Stendhal, a notable German psychologist, provides another characteristic of a free-spirited philosopher. He says, "To be a good philosopher, one must be clear, straightforward, and without illusions. A successful banker has some of the qualities needed for philosophical discoveries – the ability to see things clearly for what they are."

Test of Independence

Nietzsche says that an individual with a free spirit should undergo a test to see if they are fit to be independent and possess leadership capabilities. But he also cautions that it needs to be done at the right time, for they are risky and dangerous. He puts forth an idea that this is a test for ourselves, with us alone being the judges of the outcomes.

The first of the tests says that we shouldn't cling too tightly to anyone, not even our dearest loved ones. This is because, though we love those people dearly, they present a form of confinement (not in the bad sense but a more metaphorical one). The same goes for our homeland as well, since there is every opportunity to seek greener pastures in foreign lands. We must not get too clingy to our motherland during its toughest and the best of times, and instead, opt to be a neutral observer. Nietzsche says that this detachment is only on a personal level, rather than on a patriotic level. The next test we must set ourselves on is that we must not unduly sympathize with the unique struggles of higher individuals, even though it offers us insight into the challenges they face.

In the field of studies, we mustn't overly get attached to a particular field, even if we know that discoveries lie in wait that only we can unearth. We must persevere in the chosen field, but we must always hold our head high and let go when it is time. Next, we must also not actively pursue distant horizons, but rather let the horizon come to us. It is risky to soar higher without knowing our limits. We may end up perishing, just like Icarus burnt his waxen wings due to his own hubris.

Virtues are what make a man unique. But at the same time, some of the virtues need to be held at an arm's length. For example, charity is an excellent virtue, but it should be practiced in moderation. Excessive charity is also not a good thing, for one may end up being charitable more than their means. Also, excessive charity can also turn into a vice, like collecting donations for the poor but not following up on actual donation.

The best way to test our independence is by preserving who we are and what we do.

Free Spirit

It is unquestionable that with the glut of information available today, a philosopher or two is bound to arise in the future. But there is also true liberty present in today's world. This means that people are truly free spirits as well. People of today are destined for something that is great and fundamentally different from those who have ever existed in human history. But the point needs a slight clarification here. Each generation is only a messenger for the next generation so that the newer ones do not repeat the same mistakes we made and learn from the highs we created. Certain prejudices need to be removed if the concept of 'free spirit' needs to be retained. Globally, the term has been associated with narrow thinking and dogmatic individuals who aspire tangentially opposite to what the masses desire and lack genuine freedom. They are also said to be individuals of shallow morals and beliefs when it comes to privacy.

This outdated belief stems from the conformist age-old societal structures that are also the root cause for most of humanity's problems. True free spirit individuals, on the other hand, seek universal happiness, universal personal security, comfort, and relief for everyone. True free-spirited individuals are the champions of ideas like equal rights. They sympathize and empathize with those who suffer, and in the process think that all forms of suffering must be eradicated for humanity to progress.

It is time we changed our ways of thinking. Humanity is currently thriving in the greatest period of peace and prosperity that we have ever known, after years of hardship and challenging conditions. We have always let adversities spur our creativity, shrewdness, and resilience. Now it is time to use the ways of peace and prosperity to foster our thinking as well. We are distinctly different from the 'free-thinkers' of the past, in the sense that we need not always be so forthcoming about the source of our ideas and the ideas themselves. We just need to put them into action.

As humans, we are naturally inquisitive, sometimes to the point of ruthlessness, in our pursuit of knowledge; ever-ready for adventures and possess an abundance of free will. Our inner worlds are complex and challenging to decipher. Ultimately, we are lovers of solitude, profound introspection, and deep contemplation. We resemble night owls who tirelessly work through the darkness, and we hold our solitude in the highest regard. We might seem unconventional or even eccentric, but that's because we are individuals who cherish the profound moments of solitude, all the while retaining our free will. And perhaps our future generations might also share some of these traits.

Chapter 9

Prejudices of Philosophers

Prejudice is a burden that confuses the past, threatens the future, and renders the present inaccessible

—Maya Angelou

Prejudices wield a profound influence on human cognition. It penetrates into the deepest recesses of our minds and shapes our interactions with the world. They are not passive constructs that sit quietly in one corner of our cognition. Rather, they are active agents that constantly mould and remould our mental landscapes. On a daily basis, we encounter prejudice in innumerable forms. It lurks in the assumptions we make about people based on their appearance, background, or accent. It whispers in the stereotypes we perpetuate, whether through casual conversation, media consumption, or social media scrolling. It taints our judgments, leading us to favour certain individuals over others without even realizing it.

In a way, prejudices are like tinted lenses through which we view reality. Each person possesses their own unique set of lenses. Rather than being uniform, these individual lenses are multifaceted and shaped by a myriad of factors, including cultural upbringing, personal experiences, and societal norms.

What makes prejudices particularly insidious is their ability to operate beneath the surface of awareness. Often, we may not even recognize the extent to which our judgments are shaped by our preconceived notions. They lurk in the shadows of our subconscious, subtly guiding our perceptions and behaviour without our explicit consent. It is this unconscious influence that makes prejudices so difficult to overcome as they silently steer us down familiar pathways, constraining the range of possibilities we consider and blinding us to alternative perspectives. The impact of prejudices extends far beyond individual cognition; they are deeply woven into the fabric of social interactions and collective consciousness. Consider, for instance, how stereotypes and stigmas can seep into our perceptions of others, subtly influencing the way we interpret their words and actions. Whether it's the automatic association of certain traits with particular social groups or the reflexive attribution of motives based on superficial characteristics, these cognitive shortcuts shape our interpersonal dynamics and determine our interactions with others. From hiring practices to criminal justice proceedings, bias can taint the ostensibly objective machinery of institutions, perpetuating systemic inequalities and reinforcing existing power structures.

Prejudices are not merely irrational biases, but manifestations of power dynamics and cultural constructs. What is often labelled as 'prejudice' is a reflection of the dominant values and perspectives of a particular society or group. Prejudices are not accidental or arbitrary, but are intentionally constructed to serve the interests of those in power. They represent the imposition of a particular set of values in reality and shape human thoughts and behaviours according to the whims of the ruling class or cultural elite. In this view, prejudices are mechanisms of control.

Unconscious Biases

Have you ever found yourself in a heated debate, passionately arguing for your values as though they were undeniable truths? We must be cautious against such certainty, as we often attempt to elevate our subjective beliefs to the status of universal absolutes. But how often do we pause to consider the origins of our convictions? It is tempting to construct elaborate philosophical frameworks to rationalize and legitimize our values. Let's delve deeper into the foundations of human thought and explore what influences our unconscious biases and prejudices on philosophical interpretation. Our cultural, social, and personal backgrounds profoundly shape our understanding of abstract concepts like morality, truth, and reality. Imagine two individuals: one hails from a society valuing individual autonomy above all, while the other emerges from a collectivist culture emphasizing social harmony and communal obligation. Each individual, without even realizing it, filters their philosophical reflections through the lens of their upbringing and cultural milieu. For the former, morality might be intricately tied to personal freedom, while for the latter, it might pivot on maintaining the social fabric. Thus, the assumption of objective and universal philosophical claims must be challenged as ideas are not immutable truths but rather reflections of the unique perspectives and experiences of the individuals who conceive them.

What may seem paradoxical is that philosophers themselves are not immune to prejudices that shape their philosophical views. In fact, many philosophers are deeply influenced by the cultural milieu in which they are situated. Cultural norms, values, and traditions serve as the backdrop against which philosophical ideas are formulated and interpreted. The philosophical ideas that emerge in a particular historical period are often responses to the pressing concerns and challenges of that time, whether it be political upheaval, social change, or scientific advancements. Thus, like all thinkers, philosophers are products of their time and society. Their philosophies often reflect the prevailing attitudes, beliefs, and social structures of the eras in which they lived. While the world outside affects the thinking, the world within is also a deterministic factor. Philosophers' personal experiences and individual biographies also exert a profound influence on their philosophical outlook. Personal traumas, triumphs, and idiosyncrasies can skew one's perception of reality and shape philosophical inclinations.

The prejudice of their thoughts shines through the very work of many eminent philosophers. Immanuel Kant's philosophy is deeply entrenched in the Enlightenment period, which emphasized reason, individualism, and the pursuit of knowledge. However, Kant's views on race and gender were reflective of the biases of his time. He held views that are now considered racist, arguing that certain races were inherently inferior to others. Additionally, Kant's conception of morality, while ground-breaking in many respects, was limited by the societal norms, which often relegated women to subordinate roles.

Similarly, the philosophical ideas unfurled by Georg Wilhelm Friedrich Hegel were highly influenced by the societal structures of early nineteenth-century Europe. He conceptualized history as a dialectical process driven by the clash of opposing forces, leading to progress over time. Hegel's view of history was Eurocentric and hierarchical. He opined that European civilization was the pinnacle of human development. This Eurocentrism reflected the colonial attitudes prevalent in Hegel's time. John Stuart Mill was a proponent of utilitarianism and liberal political theory, advocating for individual liberty and the greatest happiness principle. However, Mill's views on women's rights were still limited by the Victorian norms of his time.

Martin Heidegger's philosophy, particularly his existentialism and phenomenology, was deeply influenced by the socio-political context of early twentieth-century Germany. He was briefly a member of the Nazi party and expressed anti-Semitic views in private correspondence, though the extent to which his philosophy is inherently anti-Semitic remains a subject of debate among scholars. Nonetheless, Heidegger's association with Nazism raises questions about the influence of political ideology on philosophical thought.

The rise of industrialization, nihilism, and the decline of traditional religious beliefs in Europe certainly influenced Nietzsche's thinking to some extent. But his concept of the '*Übermensch*' is often seen as more reflective of his internal philosophical struggles and personal experiences. His life was marked by existential and psychological turmoil, a journey punctuated by intense reflections on suffering, meaning, and the fundamental nature of existence. His philosophical inquiries weren't detached academic exercises but rather intimate engagements with his inner conflicts and aspirations. The Übermensch emerges as a central theme in Nietzsche's work, which represents an ideal of personal liberation and self-actualization. This concept isn't merely a response to external societal pressures; it is an expression of Nietzsche's quest for transcendence and empowerment. It symbolizes a radical revaluation of traditional values and norms. It urges us to break free from societal constraints and embrace our unique potential. In many ways, Nietzsche's concept of the Übermensch mirrors his own journey toward self-discovery and authenticity. The Übermensch, then, becomes a projection of Nietzsche's longing for personal transformation and his vision of a humanity liberated from the shackles of outdated norms and beliefs. While external factors certainly shaped Nietzsche's intellectual milieu, his concept of the Übermensch reflects a deeply personal and introspective exploration of the human condition. It is an embodiment of his philosophical rebellion against the status quo and his relentless quest for purpose in a world stripped of traditional certainties.

Many philosophers have attempted to justify their own values to impose their subjective perspectives onto others. When we attempt to elevate our subjective values to the status of universal truths, we risk imposing our perspectives onto others without acknowledging the inherent subjectivity and contingency of their beliefs. This tendency to construct elaborate philosophical systems to rationalize personal values can be seen as a form of intellectual hubris, wherein we seek to validate our preferences by cloaking them in the guise of objective truth. One of the dangers is by proclaiming one's values as universal truths, there is a tendency to dismiss alternative perspectives and marginalize dissenting voices. This can lead to a homogenization of thought and a reluctance to entertain new ideas or challenge existing norms. Besides, the imposition of personal values as universal truths can contribute to social injustices, with leaders overlooking the perspectives and needs of marginalized groups. This can perpetuate systems of oppression and hinder efforts towards social justice and equality.

Instead of attempting to justify personal values, it is more productive to recognize the inherently subjective nature of values and engage in open dialogue and debate. By acknowledging the diversity of human experience and the multiplicity of perspectives, we can cultivate empathy, tolerance, and understanding towards others. This requires a willingness to question one's own assumptions. Ultimately, the journey toward understanding the contingent and subjective nature of values is a deeply personal one. It requires introspection, self-awareness, and a willingness to challenge our own assumptions. So, as you reflect on your own values and beliefs, critically check your temptation to impose personal truths on the world.

Rethinking Truth and Reality

Perspectivism asserts that all knowledge is subjective. The idea suggests there is no universally valid perspective from which reality or truth can be judged objectively. Instead, it encourages recognition of the diversity of human perspectives and experiences. The rejection of objective truth stems from scepticism towards the notion of a universal standpoint from which reality can be grasped. Traditional attempts in philosophy to establish such an objective perspective, be it through reason, empirical observation, or metaphysical speculation, are seen as ultimately futile and illusory. Instead, our understanding of the world is inherently shaped by our unique perspective, influenced by cultural background, personal experiences, and psychological predispositions.

The pursuit of objective truth is often regarded as a manifestation of what can be termed as 'the will to truth' – a deeply ingrained desire to seek certainty and stability in understanding the world. However, this pursuit is deemed fundamentally flawed as it assumes the existence of a fixed, unchanging reality that can be known independently of human interpretation. Reality is dynamic and multifaceted and defies capture in its entirety.

Rather than striving for an unattainable objective truth, the emphasis must be on acknowledging the diversity of human perspectives and experiences. We must embrace their subjective viewpoints. The implications of this perspectivism for our understanding of truth and reality are profound. It challenges the traditional division between subjectivity and objectivity, suggesting they are not mutually exclusive but rather interdependent aspects of the human experience. Objectivity, from this viewpoint, can be seen as a form of collective subjectivity, shaped by the shared assumptions, values, and beliefs of a particular culture or community. This idea sheds light on the political dimension of knowledge, revealing how power dynamics influence the production and dissemination of truth claims. Dominant social groups often impose their perspectives, marginalizing alternative viewpoints and reinforcing existing power structures.

Yet, this perspectivism also offers opportunities for creativity, innovation, and self-expression. We are liberated from the confines of dogma and tradition, allowing for greater experimentation and diversity of thought. Instead of passively seeking pre-existing truths, there's an invitation to actively create our own truths, drawing upon our unique experiences and perspectives.

This dynamic perspective is not without its challenges and criticisms. Some argue it leads to epistemic relativism and blurs the distinction between truth and falsehood. Others highlight its neglect of the social and historical dimensions of knowledge, overlooking how power structures shape our understanding of the world. Furthermore, the rejection of objective truth raises questions about the possibility of meaningful communication and dialogue between individuals with different perspectives. Without a common standard to judge the validity of competing truth claims, resolving disagreements or reaching consensus becomes a daunting task. And if each individual's perspective is shaped by their own unique experiences and biases, genuine understanding between people may seem elusive. Despite these challenges, perspectivism continues to provoke and inspire thinkers across disciplines. It challenges us to reconsider our assumptions about truth and reality and urges us to embrace the complexity of human experience. In a world where certainty and stability are often elusive, perspectivism offers a reminder of the richness and plurality of the human condition.

Intertwined with this concept of perspectivism is the rejection of dogmatic thinking. Rather than adhering blindly to rigid frameworks imposed by tradition or authority, a more open-ended and flexible approach to philosophy is necessary – one that embraces uncertainty and ambiguity. Dogma, whether religious, philosophical, or cultural, operates as a set of unquestionable truths that are imposed upon us without room for doubt or inquiry. This imposition of fixed beliefs not only limits our freedom of thought but also hinders our exploration of new ideas and possibilities. Dogmatic thinking fosters complacency and conformity, discouraging us from challenging prevailing norms. By accepting dogma uncritically, people relinquish autonomy and become passive recipients of predetermined truths. This surrender to dogmatic authority perpetuates power dynamics, sustaining oppressive social structures. In contrast, embracing uncertainty and the inherent ambiguity of existence helps in recognizing the multifaceted and dynamic nature of reality.

The rejection of dogmatic thinking does not entail a wholesale dismissal of belief or ideology. Rather, it calls for a critical reassessment of one's beliefs and a willingness to challenge them in light of new evidence or insights. This process of intellectual self-examination is essential for intellectual and moral development. It requires courage and self-confidence. It involves confronting the uncertainties and ambiguities of existence without the comfort of absolute truths; essential for true intellectual and spiritual growth.

Individualistic Approach

Imagine a world without individualism – a world where conformity reigns supreme, and the uniqueness of human diversity is stifled. In such a world, creativity would be constrained, innovation would stagnate, and personal growth would be non-existent. Without the freedom to explore our individual passions and pursue our own paths, society would be deprived of richness and vitality.

It is only through individual thinking and an individualistic approach that the vibrant mosaic of human existence finds its true colours. In practice, the individualistic approach manifests in myriad ways. We are free to express ourselves through various forms of artistic expression – whether it be painting, music, literature, or performance art. Through these creative endeavours, we can transcend the limitations of language and communicate the depths of our innermost thoughts and emotions to the world. Similarly, the individualistic approach fuels intellectual exploration, and inspires us to question the status quo, challenge conventional wisdom, and push the boundaries of human knowledge. From scientific research and philosophical inquiry to technological innovation and academic scholarship, the pursuit of knowledge is driven by the relentless curiosity and thirst for understanding that characterizes the individualistic mind-set. But perhaps most importantly, the individualistic approach informs the cultivation of personal relationships, where we are encouraged to form authentic connections, rather than conforming to societal expectations or external pressures, we are free to forge meaningful relationships that serve as a source of support, companionship, and personal growth.

At the core of the individualistic approach lies the belief that each person possesses unique experiences, desires, and goals that warrant respect and consideration. Philosophers like John Stuart Mill championed individualism, advocating for personal liberties and the pursuit of happiness free from undue interference by external authorities. In Mill's seminal work *On Liberty*, he famously defended the principle of individual sovereignty. He argued that society should only limit individual actions when they harm others. Individualism permeates various philosophical domains, from ethics and politics to metaphysics and epistemology. In ethics, for instance, individualistic theories such as ethical egoism propose that individuals ought to act in their own self-interest, prioritizing their own well-being above all else. Political philosophies like libertarianism advocate for minimal government intervention, championing individual rights and laissez-faire capitalism.

Concurrently, herd mentality – which is nothing but the unquestioning adherence to societal norms and values at the expense of personal autonomy and authenticity – must be harshly criticized. It's necessary to call for the cultivation of one's unique identity and will to power, the drive for self-expression and self-overcoming. The idea of a universal human nature or essence must always be rejected, emphasizing instead the radical uniqueness of each individual. There are no inherent moral truths or values; rather, morality is a product of human creativity and will. This perspective challenges the idea of individual rights and liberties as universally applicable. However, true individuality doesn't arise from isolation but from engagement with others and with the world, contrasting with the atomistic individualism that characterizes much of modern Western thought.

***

Chapter 10

History of Morals

Morality is not the doctrine of how we may make ourselves happy, but how we may make ourselves worthy of happiness

—Immanuel Kant

Morality stands as one of the defining threads in the grand tapestry of human evolution, weaving its way through the fabric of societies and shaping the course of history. Yet, beneath the veneer of moral righteousness lies a labyrinth of hidden motives, power struggles, and conflicting agendas. In this chapter, we shall unveil the facade of conventional morality, exposing the raw genealogy of morals beneath.

At the outset, let's conduct a genealogical investigation into the tangled roots of our ethical frameworks, tracing their development through the annals of human history. What emerges is a narrative of power dynamics, societal tensions, and existential struggles, challenging us to re-evaluate our most cherished beliefs about right and wrong. Morality is not a fixed standard imposed from above, but a dynamic and contingent phenomenon shaped by human psychology and cultural forces.

The role of resentment in the formation of moral values is a key insight that we must grasp. Moral codes often emerge as a response to power imbalances and injustices. They serve as a tool for the oppressed to assert their moral superiority over their oppressors. Take, for instance, the values of humility and meekness celebrated in slave morality. These virtues can be seen as a form of psychological warfare against the dominance of the ruling class. By embracing such virtues, the oppressed undermine the legitimacy of their oppressors and stake a claim to a higher moral ground. Furthermore, the genealogical approach reveals the fluid and contingent nature of moral concepts. What is deemed virtuous or sinful in one culture or era may be viewed quite differently in another. This challenges the notion of moral absolutism and underscores the constructed nature of morality. Moral values are not timeless and immutable truths; they are contingent upon historical context and subject to change over time.

However, our exploration isn't merely a deconstruction of moral systems; it is a call to action. By uncovering the hidden motivations and power dynamics behind our ethical beliefs, we are challenged to question the authority of traditional moral codes and reclaim agency over our ethical lives. We are invited to engage in a process of critical reflection and self-examination, interrogating the sources of our moral values and scrutinizing the agendas that shape them. In the light of our genealogy, we are faced with a profound challenge: to transcend the limitations of traditional morality and forge a more authentic and self-affirming ethic. This requires us to move beyond passive acceptance of inherited moral codes and instead cultivate values that resonate with our own deepest aspirations and desires. It's a call to embrace our own agency and responsibility, to affirm the inherent worth and dignity of all individuals.

As we delve deeper into our exploration of the genealogy of morals, let us heed the call to question, to challenge, and to reimagine the very foundations of our ethical lives. Only by confronting the uncomfortable truths about the origins and motivations behind our moral beliefs can we hope to transcend the limitations of conventional morality and embrace a more liberated and authentic ethic grounded in the affirmation of life.

The Genealogy of Morality

To understand the genealogy of morality, we must first acknowledge its roots in the four pillars of human knowledge viz., anthropology, sociology, psychology, and philosophy. From an anthropological perspective, morality can be seen as a set of norms, values, and beliefs that govern social behaviour within a group or society. These moral codes often evolve over time in response to various factors, such as cultural changes, technological advancements, and environmental pressures. Another approach to exploring the genealogy of morality is through the lens of evolutionary psychology. Evolutionary psychologists propose that moral behaviours, such as cooperation, altruism, and reciprocity, have emerged in humans as adaptive strategies for survival and reproduction. Through processes like natural selection, individuals who exhibited these behaviours were more likely to thrive and pass on their genes to future generations. Social psychologists have investigated the role of socialization and cultural transmission in shaping moral values and beliefs. From a young age, individuals are socialized into their respective cultures through interactions with family members, peers, and other social institutions. These interactions instil certain moral principles and norms that guide individuals' behaviour and influence their moral judgments. Philosophically, the genealogy of morality raises questions about the nature of moral values, their origins, and their justification. Moral philosophers have debated whether moral principles are objective truths that exist independently of human societies or whether they are socially constructed conventions that vary across cultures and contexts.

This debate has profound implications for how we understand and evaluate moral beliefs and practices.

We encounter various historical and cultural influences that have shaped moral thought. For example, religious traditions have played a significant role in shaping moral values and beliefs in many societies throughout history. Religious texts and teachings often provide moral frameworks and guidelines for adherents to follow, influencing their behaviour and ethical decision-making. Additionally, political ideologies and systems of governance have also influenced the development of morality within societies. For instance, authoritarian regimes may impose certain moral codes on their citizens through laws and regulations, while democratic societies may prioritize individual rights and freedoms as foundational moral principles. Furthermore, economic factors such as wealth distribution, resource scarcity, and labour relations can also impact moral values and attitudes within societies.

Economic inequalities, for example, may give rise to debates about social justice, leading to the emergence of moral movements advocating for change. In recent centuries, advances in science and technology have introduced new ethical dilemmas with issues such as genetic engineering, artificial intelligence, and environmental degradation, raising profound questions about our responsibilities to future generations and the broader ecosystem.

In this exploration of genealogy of morality, we have to depart from the conventional philosophical methods that typically focus on abstract metaphysical speculation. Instead, we need to engage with the historical, psychological, and anthropological dimensions of moral concepts. From ancient civilizations to modern societies, the evolution of moral thought has been a dynamic process, reflecting the diverse perspectives and values inherent within human nature. One notable examination of this evolution comes from the concept of slave vs master morality which provides insight into the divergent paths taken by different societies in their pursuit of virtue and righteousness. Slave morality revolves around a morality born from a position of weakness, subjugation, or oppression. It celebrates virtues like humility, compassion, and meekness, viewing them as noble and virtuous. In this framework, good is equated with selflessness, while evil is often associated with strength, dominance, and ambition. Contrastingly, master morality originates from a position of strength, power, or superiority. It exalts qualities such as courage, ambition, and assertiveness. This dichotomy serves as a lens through which we can understand the shifting sands of ethical thought across cultures and epochs.

Master morality can be found in ancient warrior cultures, such as the Spartans of ancient Greece or the samurai of feudal Japan. In these societies, strength and prowess in battle were highly valued, and individuals were expected to demonstrate courage and honour in their actions. Warriors who exhibited these qualities were celebrated as heroes and held in high esteem by their peers. The Spartan warrior ethos emphasized discipline, bravery, and self-sacrifice for the greater good of the community. Spartans were trained from a young age to endure hardship and excel in combat. The ideal Spartan warrior embodied the virtues of master morality, demonstrating strength, courage, and a willingness to assert dominance over their enemies. Similarly, the Samurai of feudal Japan adhered to a code of conduct known as 'bushido', which emphasized loyalty, honour, and self-discipline. Samurai were expected to devote themselves fully to their lord and to be willing to lay down their lives in his service. Acts of bravery and self-sacrifice were celebrated in samurai culture, and those who exemplified these virtues were revered as exemplars of master morality. In both of these cases, master morality is rooted in a sense of pride and self-confidence, as well as a willingness to assert dominance over others.

Early Christianity serves as a quintessential example of slave morality in action. In the teachings of Jesus Christ and the early Christian community, humility, compassion, and forgiveness are exalted as virtues. Concepts such as turning the other cheek, loving one's enemies, and the meek inheriting the earth emphasize the moral superiority of those who endure suffering with grace and dignity. This moral framework found resonance among early Christians who often faced persecution and marginalization under the Roman Empire. By embracing values rooted in empathy and selflessness, they sought to find strength and meaning in their struggles, turning adversity into a testament of their faith.

The Civil Rights Movement in the United States provides another powerful illustration of slave morality in practice. Led by figures like Martin Luther King Jr, the movement championed nonviolent resistance and passive resistance as a means of confronting systemic racism and oppression. Through acts of peaceful protest, sit-ins, and marches, activists sought to challenge the status quo while embodying principles of love, equality, and justice. By refusing to retaliate in the face of violence and hatred, they asserted their moral superiority, ultimately paving the way for legislative reforms and social change. Mahatma Gandhi's philosophy of satyagraha, or 'truth force', offers a compelling example of slave morality in action. Through campaigns of non-violent resistance and civil disobedience, Gandhi sought to confront and transform injustice without resorting to violence or hatred. His emphasis on moral integrity, self-sacrifice, and compassion empowered the oppressed to reclaim their dignity and challenge the moral legitimacy of colonial rule. By embodying principles of humility and empathy, Gandhi inspired a movement that transcended the confines of political power, mobilizing ordinary people to uphold the moral principles of truth and justice.

Humanitarian aid organizations such as the Red Cross and Doctors without Borders exemplify slave morality through their commitment to alleviating suffering and promoting human dignity. These organizations provide assistance to communities affected by conflict, disaster, and poverty, regardless of nationality, religion, or political affiliation. By extending a helping hand to the most vulnerable, humanitarian aid workers embody the moral imperative to alleviate suffering and uphold the inherent worth of every individual. Movements advocating for animal rights and welfare also draw upon principles of slave morality by emphasizing empathy, compassion, and the moral obligation to protect sentient beings. Activists who protest against animal cruelty recognize the inherent value and rights of all living creatures. Through their actions, they challenge the prevailing notion of human superiority and advocate for a more inclusive ethic that extends compassion and care to all sentient beings, regardless of species.

In today's world, the echoes of slave and master morality resonate across various facets of society, influencing individual behaviour, societal norms, and even political ideologies. Left-leaning movements often emphasize equality, social justice, and compassion, echoing the sentiments of slave morality. Conversely, right-wing ideologies frequently prioritize individual liberty, meritocracy, and strength, mirroring the principles of master morality. Corporate cultures that prioritize competition, assertiveness, and ambition reflect the values of master morality, rewarding those who exhibit dominance and strategic prowess. Conversely, initiatives focused on social responsibility, sustainability, and ethical business practices align more closely with the principles of slave morality, emphasizing empathy and collective well-being over individual gain.

Central to this analysis is the role of language in shaping our moral concepts and judgments. Language, far from being a neutral medium, operates through a series of metaphors deeply embedded in our cultural and linguistic frameworks. These metaphors are not arbitrary; they encapsulate particular ways of perceiving and understanding the world. Language thus becomes a powerful tool – not just reflecting pre-existing truths, but actively creating and shaping our reality and our values. By digging into the historical development of moral concepts, we can trace their origins back to these linguistic roots. What we often take as rational moral judgments are, in reality, the result of long-standing historical processes. The metaphors embedded in language guide our interpretations and shape our moral landscape. This perspective reveals that moral judgments are less about universal rational principles and more about the historical and cultural contexts from which they emerge.

The Illusion of Moral Absolutism

Morality is not a fixed standard imposed from some transcendent realm, but rather a fluid and contingent phenomenon shaped by the interplay of human psychology and cultural forces. This perspective flies in the face of centuries of religious and philosophical tradition, which have often posited moral principles as immutable laws emanating from a divine source. Traditional moral codes are products of human interpretation – interpretations that are heavily influenced by prevailing power structures and cultural norms.

Likewise, moral values are not universal but rather contingent upon the particularities of a given society and its historical context. Consider the practice of polygamy in different societies. In some cultures, having multiple spouses is considered morally acceptable or even virtuous, while in others it is condemned as immoral or illegal. This discrepancy highlights the relativity of moral values, as what is deemed acceptable varies greatly depending on cultural norms and traditions. This relativistic view of morality challenges the notion of moral absolutes and suggests that what is deemed morally right or wrong is subject to change over time and across different social and cultural contexts.

Moreover, traditional moral codes are often used as instruments of power and control by those in positions of authority. Religious and political leaders often use moral values as devices of manipulation to justify their own dominance and suppress dissent. This manipulation serves to reinforce existing power structures and perpetuate the status quo. An example of political manipulation of moral values can be seen in propaganda campaigns that demonize certain groups or ideologies as morally reprehensible. For instance, during times of war or political unrest, governments often portray their adversaries as evil or subhuman in order to rally support for their cause and justify acts of aggression. Throughout history, colonial powers have often justified their conquests and exploitation of other cultures by invoking moral principles such as the 'civilizing mission' or the spread of Christianity. However, these moral justifications are merely masks for the exercise of power and domination over others, serving to perpetuate the interests of the colonizers rather than genuinely moral aims.

Over time, societies often undergo shifts in their moral attitudes and values. One of the most striking examples of this phenomenon can be observed in the evolution of attitudes towards gender equality. In many traditional societies, patriarchal norms dictated strict gender roles and hierarchies, relegating women to subordinate positions in both the public and private spheres. However, over time, movements for women's rights and gender equality have challenged these entrenched norms, leading to significant social and legal reforms aimed at promoting gender equity and empowering women. Today, many societies recognize the importance of gender equality as a fundamental human right, reflecting a profound shift in moral consciousness and societal values. Similarly, attitudes towards LGBTQ+ rights have undergone dramatic changes in recent decades, reflecting a growing recognition of the rights and dignity of individuals regardless of their sexual orientation or gender identity. Historically, LGBTQ+ individuals have faced widespread discrimination, persecution, and violence. However, through tireless advocacy and activism, LGBTQ+ communities have made significant strides towards achieving legal recognition, protection from discrimination, and societal acceptance. These changes signify a fundamental shift in moral attitudes, as societies increasingly embrace principles of inclusivity, diversity, and respect for individual autonomy.

Similarly, the emergence of environmental consciousness has spurred a revaluation of humanity's relationship with the natural world and the ethical implications of environmental degradation. In the face of escalating environmental crises such as climate change, deforestation, and pollution, there has been a growing realization of the interconnectedness of ecological systems and the urgent need for sustainable stewardship of the planet. This shift in moral consciousness has led to a proliferation of environmental movements and policies aimed at promoting conservation, biodiversity, and environmental justice, reflecting a broader recognition of our collective responsibility to protect the earth and ensure the well-being of present and future generations.

As society progresses, our understanding of morality continues to evolve, challenging long-held assumptions and revealing the constructed nature of moral frameworks. The illusion of moral absolutism begins to fade as we recognize the complexities of human experience and the diversity of moral perspectives that exist within and across cultures. By embracing a more nuanced understanding of morality – one that acknowledges its fluidity, contingency, and cultural specificity – we open ourselves to the possibility of genuine moral progress and the realization of a more just and compassionate world.

The Transvaluation of Values

Traditional norms and expectations regarding gender roles and identities are continually being challenged and redefined. Movements advocating for LGBTQ+ rights and recognition have led to a broader acceptance and celebration of diverse expressions of gender and sexuality. This represents a profound 'transvaluation of values', where outdated notions of binary gender and heteronormativity are giving way to more inclusive and fluid understandings of identity. Another example can be found in economics and capitalism. The traditional emphasis on profit maximization and material wealth is being scrutinized in light of growing concerns over income inequality, environmental degradation, and social justice. Alternative economic models, such as sustainable development and social entrepreneurship, prioritize values of community, environmental stewardship, and equitable distribution of resources. This reflects a broader transvaluation of economic values, where the pursuit of profit is no longer seen as the sole measure of success.

Transvaluation challenges the traditional notions of good and evil, right and wrong, by proposing a radical revaluation of our ethical and moral frameworks. This concept emerged in the late nineteenth century, amidst a backdrop of profound societal and intellectual upheaval. The decline of religious authority, the rise of scientific rationalism, and the erosion of traditional moral certainties created fertile ground for this revolutionary idea to take root. Over the decades, transvaluation of values continued to resonate with the masses and evolve alongside human values. They found expression in various intellectual movements, from existentialism to postmodernism, each offering its own interpretation and critique.

As humanity stands at the threshold of a new era, marked by unprecedented technological advancements, shifting global dynamics, and profound social transformations, the imperative to forge a new regime of moral principles has never been more pressing. The traditional moral frameworks are increasingly being called into question, challenged by the complexities of the modern world and the diverse array of ethical dilemmas they present. The call to action is clear: it is time to chart a new course, grounded in the recognition of our shared humanity and the imperative to cultivate values that foster genuine flourishing and well-being for all humanity. At the heart of this endeavour lies a fundamental revaluation of our ethical foundations. This requires us to transcend the narrow confines of binary thinking – of good versus evil, right versus wrong – and instead embrace the complexities and nuances of moral experience. It demands a willingness to engage in critical reflection and dialogue, to confront uncomfortable truths about the origins of our moral beliefs, and to acknowledge the inherent diversity of human experience.

Central to this new morality is the recognition of moral agency – the capacity of individuals to shape their own ethical lives and contribute to the collective project of building a more just and compassionate society. This entails moving beyond passive adherence to inherited moral codes and instead cultivating a deep sense of responsibility for the impact of our actions on others and the world around us. It requires us to strive for authenticity and integrity in our ethical commitments, guided by a commitment to truth, empathy, and solidarity with the marginalized and oppressed.

Moreover, a new morality must be grounded in a robust understanding of human flourishing, informed by insights from psychology, neuroscience, and the social sciences. It must recognize that true well-being encompasses not only material prosperity, but also psychological, emotional, and spiritual fulfilment. It acknowledges the importance of fostering strong social bonds, nurturing meaningful relationships, and cultivating a sense of purpose and belonging. At its core, this new morality is rooted in the affirmation of life – the recognition of the inherent dignity and worth of every human being, and the commitment to creating conditions that enable all individuals to thrive and fulfil their potential.

In the quest for a new morality, we must also grapple with the profound ethical challenges posed by emerging technologies and the rapid pace of globalization. From artificial intelligence and genetic engineering to climate change and geopolitical instability, these forces are reshaping the very fabric of human existence. In confronting these challenges, we are called upon to uphold timeless moral principles – such as justice, equality, and solidarity – while also adapting our ethical frameworks to address the unique demands of the digital age.

***

Chapter 11

Virtues

Virtue is its own reward.

—Cicero

Virtues, much like the flora of a garden, are the qualities that flourish within us and shape our character. They are the seeds planted in the fertile ground of our hearts, nurtured by wisdom and experience, and pruned by the trials of life. Just as a gardener must diligently care for the plants, so too must we consciously foster our virtues, allowing them to grow strong and resilient. In the literal sense, virtue refers to a moral quality deemed to be good or desirable in a person. It is adherence to principles of right and wrong, but often based on societal norms, ethical codes, or religious beliefs.

Cardinal virtues originate from classical antiquity and have played a significant role in both philosophical and religious traditions. The four cardinal virtues are prudence, justice, fortitude, and temperance. Prudence involves practical wisdom and the ability to make sound judgments, guiding other virtues by setting rules and measures. It requires an understanding of moral principles and the foresight to judge the consequences of actions. Justice is the virtue concerned with giving each person their due and ensuring fair treatment and respect for individuals' rights and responsibilities. Fortitude, or courage, enables individuals to face challenges, endure difficulties, and overcome obstacles with a steadfast spirit. Temperance moderates attraction to pleasures and regulates desires and appetites, promoting self-control and balance to avoid excess and indulgence. Theological virtues are central to Christian ethics and are believed to be gifts from God, infused into the soul to guide spiritual and moral life. These virtues – faith, hope, and charity or love – are foundational in the teachings of the New Testament. Moral virtues are habits or dispositions that enable individuals to act according to reason and moral law, developed through practice and repetition. Intellectual virtues are qualities of the mind that enable individuals to pursue and appreciate truth and knowledge, essential for critical thinking, learning, and the development of wisdom. These virtues include characteristics such as curiosity, open-mindedness, intellectual humility, and critical thinking.

Cultivating virtues is essential for leading a good and fulfilling life, and that they contribute to personal character development and positive interactions with others. The concept of virtue, or '*areté*' in Greek, finds its earliest formal articulation in the works of ancient philosophers such as Socrates, Plato, and Aristotle. For Socrates, virtue was synonymous with knowledge; to know the good is to do the good. This intellectualist view posited that moral failings were merely the result of ignorance. Plato expanded on his mentor's ideas, presenting a tripartite soul in *The Republic* where virtues aligned with different parts of the soul: wisdom with reason, courage with spirit, and temperance with appetite. Aristotle, however, provided the most comprehensive ancient account of virtues in his *Nicomachean Ethics.* He introduced the doctrine of the mean, asserting that virtue lies between two extremes of excess and deficiency. For instance, courage is the mean between recklessness and cowardice. Aristotle's teleological perspective emphasized that virtues enable individuals to fulfil their purpose and achieve '*eudaimonia*' or human flourishing.

Parallel to the philosophical traditions of Greece, religious texts and cultural practices across the world also laid the groundwork for understanding virtues. In Hinduism, the concept of '*dharma*' encompasses duties and ethical conduct, closely aligning with virtues such as truthfulness, non-violence, and compassion. Similarly, Confucianism in ancient China emphasized virtues like filial piety, humaneness, and righteousness as fundamental to social harmony and personal development. In the Abrahamic traditions, virtues are often framed as divine commandments or moral imperatives. The 'Ten Commandments' in Judaism, the 'Beatitudes' in Christianity, and the 'Five Pillars of Islam' provide frameworks for virtuous living that extend beyond individual behaviour to shape communal and societal norms.

The medieval period witnessed the synthesis of classical philosophy and religious doctrine, particularly within the Scholastic tradition. Thomas Aquinas, a key figure in this synthesis, integrated Aristotelian ethics with Christian theology. Aquinas delineated cardinal virtues – prudence, justice, fortitude, and temperance – complemented by theological virtues of faith, hope, and charity. This integration reinforced the view that virtues are both natural and divine, guiding individuals toward both earthly well-being and spiritual salvation.

The Renaissance era, marked by humanism and a revival of classical learning, prompted a re-evaluation of virtues. Thinkers like Erasmus and Machiavelli offered contrasting perspectives; Erasmus extolled classical virtues and moral integrity, while Machiavelli, in 'The Prince', argued for a more pragmatic approach to virtue, where the ends justify the means. This period highlighted the tension between idealism and realism in the discourse on virtues.

The Enlightenment brought a shift towards reason and individualism, which influence the conception of virtues. Philosophers such as David Hume and Immanuel Kant offered new insights. Hume viewed virtues through the lens of sentiment and social utility, emphasizing qualities like benevolence and justice as essential to human cooperation. Kant, in contrast, presented a deontological framework where virtues are derived from the categorical imperative, an absolute moral law dictated by reason. The 19th century saw further evolution with the rise of existential and postmodern thought. Nietzsche critiqued traditional virtues as manifestations of slave morality – values imposed by weaker individuals to constrain the strong.

As philosophical perspectives on virtues developed over centuries, they began to intersect with human behavioural aspects and social dynamics. This provided a novel lens through which to examine how virtues manifest in human behaviour and decision-making processes. By integrating ethical considerations into economic models, researchers began to explore the complex motivations behind human actions, challenging the notion that individuals act solely out of self-interest.

Virtues, Human Behaviour and Society

Behavioural economics studies how virtues like altruism, fairness, and trust affect individual choices and societal outcomes. Unlike traditional economics, which often assumes rational self-interest as the primary motivator, behavioural economics recognizes that people frequently act based on ethical considerations. This departure from pure self-interest can be observed in various experimental settings. For example, in the Ultimatum Game, one player proposes a division of a sum of money, and the other player can accept or reject it. Rejection means both players get nothing. Studies consistently show that people offer fair splits and reject offers perceived as unfair, even at a cost to themselves. This behaviour highlights the role of fairness and reciprocity in decision-making. Similarly, in the Public Goods Game, participants decide how much of their private tokens to put into a public pot, which is then multiplied and redistributed. Despite the incentive to free-ride (contributing nothing while benefiting from others' contributions), many people contribute, driven by a sense of collective responsibility. These experiments demonstrate that virtues like fairness, reciprocity, and altruism are crucial in guiding behaviour that promotes social welfare and cooperation, even when such behaviour contradicts self-interest. People's willingness to sacrifice their own benefits for the sake of fairness or collective good underscores the powerful influence of these virtues.

Virtues significantly shape social norms and group dynamics. Social identity theory and in-group favouritism illustrate how virtues such as loyalty and solidarity foster group cohesion and collective action. When individuals identify strongly with a group, they are more likely to act in ways that benefit the group, driven by a sense of loyalty and shared purpose. Social identity theory suggests that individuals derive a sense of self from their group memberships. Virtues like loyalty and solidarity are essential for maintaining group identity and cohesion.

In-group favouritism refers to the tendency to prefer and prioritize the needs of one's group over those of outsiders. While this can lead to positive outcomes within the group, such as enhanced cooperation and mutual support, it can also result in negative consequences like discrimination and conflict without-groups. Therefore, balancing in-group loyalty with broader ethical principles is crucial.

The absence of virtuous behaviour can lead to significant social challenges. When ethical conduct is missing, social fragmentation and conflict can arise, undermining cooperation and trust within and between groups. This fragmentation can manifest in various forms. For example, trust is fundamental for social and economic transactions. Without it, cooperation breaks down, leading to inefficiencies and increased transaction costs. In environments where trust is low, individuals and organizations may resort to costly monitoring and enforcement mechanisms to ensure compliance. Additionally, a lack of virtues such as fairness and solidarity can lead to social divisions and conflict. When individuals or groups act purely out of self-interest without regard for ethical considerations, social cohesion deteriorates.

Virtuous leadership has been a cornerstone of effective governance throughout history. The idea that leaders should embody virtues has long been a subject of contemplation and has been integral to the discourse on governance and ethics. In ancient times, the concept of virtuous leadership was foundational to the vision of a just society. Philosophers and thinkers across different cultures emphasized the necessity of moral and virtuous rulers to ensure a harmonious and prosperous community. This ideal has not only persisted through the ages but has also evolved to inform modern leadership theories that stress the importance of integrity, empathy, and accountability. Integrity is a fundamental quality of virtuous leadership. It encompasses honesty, transparency, and consistency in actions and decisions. Leaders with integrity maintain a high standard of ethical conduct and ensure their actions align with their values and principles. When leaders demonstrate integrity, they set a powerful example for their team members, encouraging them to also act with honesty and uphold ethical standards.

Empathy is another essential attribute of virtuous leadership. Empathetic leaders are attuned to the needs and concerns of their followers, which enables them to respond effectively and compassionately. This quality fosters a supportive and inclusive environment. It helps leaders to connect with their followers on a deeper level, enhancing communication and collaboration. Accountability is the third pillar of virtuous leadership. It is the responsibility of leaders to answer for their actions and decisions. Accountable leaders acknowledge their mistakes, take corrective actions, and learn from their experiences. This attitude promotes a culture of accountability within the organization, where individuals feel responsible for their contributions and are motivated to perform their best. In political systems, accountability is crucial for maintaining the legitimacy and credibility of the leadership.

The impact of virtuous leadership extends beyond the immediate context of governance and organizations. It has the potential to influence broader societal values and behaviours. Leaders serve as role models, and their actions set a precedent for others to follow. When leaders demonstrate integrity, empathy, and accountability, they encourage these qualities in their followers. This ripple effect can lead to a more ethical and compassionate society, where individuals are more likely to act with consideration for others and take responsibility for their actions. In modern contexts, ethical leadership theories have built on these timeless principles to address the complexities of contemporary governance and organizational management. These theories emphasize the importance of ethical behaviour and moral decision-making in leadership. They argue that effective leaders are not only skilled and knowledgeable, but also virtuous in their conduct. One significant aspect of modern ethical leadership is the focus on creating a positive organizational culture. Leaders are seen as the architects of the organizational environment, shaping the norms, values, and behaviours within their teams.

This cultural influence is particularly important in today's interconnected and rapidly changing world, where ethical lapses can have far-reaching consequences. Issues such as corruption, inequality, and social injustice can be effectively tackled through ethical leadership, showing that virtuous leadership is not only about guiding an organization or a political entity, but also about contributing to the common good and fostering a just society.

Civic virtues such as justice, tolerance, and civic-mindedness are fundamental to democratic societies. The emphasis on civic education and community engagement seeks to cultivate these virtues. The interconnectedness of the modern world necessitates a re-examination of virtues through a global lens. Cross-cultural psychology and intercultural communication studies reveal how different societies prioritize various virtues, yet commonalities exist that transcend cultural boundaries. For instance, virtues like honesty, compassion, and respect are universally valued, and facilitate intercultural understanding and cooperation.

Virtues in an Uncertain World

In an era marked by rapid and often unsettling changes, the concept of virtue has taken on renewed importance. Amid an atmosphere of global inequality, the role of virtues in guiding ethical action and sustainable development is more crucial than ever. Virtues like resilience, adaptability, and global citizenship are indispensable for addressing these complex issues. Resilience is a virtue that has gained prominence in response to the myriad crises of our time. It is the capacity to recover from setbacks, adapt to change, and keep going in the face of adversity. In the context of climate change, resilience involves the ability to withstand environmental disasters and also the capacity to adapt to long-term shifts in climate patterns. Communities around the world are developing resilience strategies to cope with extreme weather events, rising sea levels, and other climate-related challenges. During the COVID-19 pandemic, these virtues became paramount in guiding individual and collective actions. Compassion drove people to support each other through acts of kindness, from checking on neighbours to volunteering for community aid. Resilience helped individuals and communities adapt to the new normal, finding ways to cope with social isolation, economic hardship, and the uncertainties of the virus. Responsibility was evident in the adherence to public health guidelines, such as wearing masks, practicing social distancing, and getting vaccinated to protect not only oneself but also the broader community. These virtues, rooted in a deep sense of interconnectedness and empathy, played a crucial role in mitigating the global crisis, fostering solidarity, and promoting a collective effort to overcome the unprecedented challenges posed by the pandemic.

On a personal level, resilience is about maintaining mental and emotional strength in the face of difficulties. Cultivating resilience begins with a shift in perspective. Instead of viewing adversities as barriers, resilient individuals see them as learning experiences that can lead to greater wisdom and strength. For instance, during economic downturns or periods of job loss, a resilient person might seek out new skills or career opportunities, viewing the situation as a chance to reinvent themselves and explore new paths. Mental and emotional resilience is also supported by several practical strategies. Maintaining strong social connections provides a vital support network that individuals can rely on during tough times. Regular physical activity, mindfulness practices, and a healthy lifestyle contribute to overall well-being, making it easier to manage stress and bounce back from adversity.

Additionally, setting realistic goals and breaking them down into manageable steps can help individuals stay focused and motivated, even when faced with significant challenges. Adaptability, closely related to resilience, is another virtue that has become critical in our rapidly changing world. It refers to the ability to adjust one's attitudes, behaviours, and strategies in response to new circumstances. Technological disruption, for example, is transforming industries and economies at an unprecedented pace. Workers must continuously update their skills and knowledge to stay relevant in the job market. Companies must innovate to stay competitive, and policymakers must develop flexible regulations.

In an increasingly interconnected world, the virtue of global citizenship is essential. Global citizenship entails recognizing our shared humanity and taking responsibility for our collective well-being. It emphasizes the importance of empathy, cultural understanding, and a commitment to social justice on a global scale. Global citizenship also involves advocating for human rights and working towards a more equitable and inclusive world, fostering a sense of solidarity and cooperation amongst the human race.

Education plays a crucial role in cultivating virtues. Schools and universities are not only places for acquiring knowledge but also for developing character. Educational institutions can foster virtues by creating environments that encourage ethical reflection, critical thinking, and compassionate action. Character education programmes, for example, can teach students about the importance of virtues such as honesty, respect, and responsibility. These can help students develop the skills and dispositions needed to navigate ethical dilemmas and contribute positively to society. Moreover, education can promote global citizenship by exposing students to diverse perspectives and encouraging them to think critically about global issues, preparing students to be responsible and engaged citizens in an interconnected world.

The Evolving Nature of Virtues

The dynamic nature of virtues invites continual re-imagination and dialogue. Traditional virtues such as courage, wisdom, and justice remain important, but their application must evolve to meet contemporary needs. For instance, the virtue of courage is now understood not only as physical bravery but also as moral courage – the willingness to stand up for what is right in the face of social pressure. Wisdom involves not only knowledge, but also the ability to apply that knowledge in a nuanced and context-sensitive manner. Justice extends beyond legal fairness to include social justice, which addresses systemic inequalities and strives for a more equitable distribution of resources and opportunities.

Feminist ethics has significantly contributed to the re-imagination of virtues by challenging traditional ethical theories and practices, which often marginalized or ignored women's experiences and perspectives. This re-imagination involves not only the inclusion of women's voices but also a fundamental rethinking of what virtues are, how they are cultivated, and how they function in moral life. Traditional ethical theories have historically emphasized virtues like courage, justice, temperance, and wisdom. These virtues were often construed in ways that aligned with male-dominated social norms and roles. For example, courage was typically associated with battlefield bravery, justice with impartial and abstract principles, and temperance with self-control in a manner that neglected the complexities of everyday life.

Feminist ethicists critique these traditional conceptions for being overly individualistic, universalizing, and detached from the realities of human interdependence. They argue that such virtues, as traditionally understood, do not adequately account for the moral experiences and contributions of women, who have historically been relegated to the private sphere and whose moral labour has often been undervalued.

Feminist ethics re-imagine virtues by emphasizing relationality, care, and the social context of moral actions. This approach foregrounds the moral significance of care, empathy, and interconnectedness, which have often been overlooked or undervalued in traditional ethics. Carol Gilligan, in her groundbreaking work, *In a Different Voice*, highlighted how women's moral reasoning often revolved around care and responsibility rather than abstract principles of justice. This perspective was further developed by scholars who argued for an ethics of care that prioritizes relationality and emotional engagement over detached reasoning. In re-imagining care as a virtue, feminist ethicists emphasize its role in fostering and maintaining relationships. Care involves attentiveness, responsiveness, and a commitment to meeting the needs of others, recognizing the interdependence that characterizes human life. This reconceptualization challenges the traditional emphasis on autonomy and self-sufficiency, instead proposing that moral agents are fundamentally connected and that virtues should reflect this reality.

Empathy and compassion are also re-imagined within feminist ethics as essential virtues. Traditional ethics often viewed emotions with suspicion, valuing rationality and objectivity over emotional engagement. Feminists, however, argue that empathy and compassion are crucial for understanding others' perspectives and for fostering moral sensitivity. Empathy involves the ability to understand and share the feelings of others, which is essential for moral responsiveness and solidarity. Compassion extends this understanding into a motivation to alleviate suffering. By re-imagining these emotions as virtues, feminist ethics highlights the importance of emotional intelligence in moral life and challenges the dichotomy between reason and emotion.

The re-imagination of virtues through feminist ethics has broader implications for society and various fields, including education, healthcare, and public policy. In education, incorporating feminist ethics can promote a more inclusive and holistic approach to moral development, encouraging students to value empathy, care, and relationality alongside traditional virtues. In healthcare, feminist ethics can enhance patient care by fostering a more compassionate and context-sensitive approach to medical practice. In public policy, feminist ethics advocates for policies that recognize and address the relational and contextual dimensions of social issues. This perspective can inform more equitable and responsive policies.

The digital age presents unique challenges and opportunities for the practice of virtues. The rapid proliferation of information and communication technologies has transformed how we interact, work, and live. These changes necessitate a revaluation of traditional virtues and the development of new ones that are relevant to the digital context. Digital literacy, for example, has become a crucial virtue. It involves not only the technical skills to navigate digital platforms but also the critical thinking abilities to assess the credibility of information and the ethical considerations of digital behaviour. In an age of misinformation and digital manipulation, the virtue of truthfulness is more important than ever. Another emerging virtue is digital empathy, which involves understanding and responding to the emotions and experiences of others in online interactions. Digital empathy can help mitigate the negative effects of online anonymity and reduce cyberbullying and harassment.

***

Chapter 12

What is Considered Noble?

The highest nobility lies in taming the fury of your soul

—Rick Riordan

Nobility is the luminous essence of the human spirit, a symphony of virtues harmonized into a life of purpose and grace. It is the quiet strength that stands firm in the face of adversity, the gentle hand that lifts others up, and the steadfast heart that beats with integrity and compassion. Nobility is not bestowed by birth-right but earned through the deliberate cultivation of character, the pursuit of wisdom, and the unwavering commitment to justice. At its core, nobility is the art of elevated being – a transcendence of selfish desires and mundane concerns, reaching towards the sublime heights of what it means to be truly human. It is found in the courage to act with conviction, the humility to acknowledge one's limitations, and the generosity to share one's gifts with the world. Like a beacon in the night, nobility guides us towards a life of meaningful connection, enduring impact, and profound inner peace. In our quest to comprehend the meaning of nobility, we must surpass mere definitions and probe into the essence of what makes actions and character truly noble. Nobility can be seen as the pinnacle of human moral development, where one's actions and intentions align with higher principles of good. Nobility reflects a holistic integration of character, intellect, and spirit aimed at the betterment of oneself and society.

The Stoics, ancient philosophers such as Epictetus and Marcus Aurelius, offered insights into the nature of nobility through the lens of inner virtue and resilience. For the Stoics, nobility is found in the strength of character and the mastery over one's inner life. They believed that true nobility arises from living in accordance with nature and reason, maintaining equanimity in the face of life's trials. Marcus Aurelius, in his *Meditations*, encapsulates this view: 'Waste no more time arguing about what a good man should be. Be one.' Here, nobility is not an external accolade but an internal state of being, characterized by wisdom, self-control, and an unwavering commitment to virtue. The Stoic noble individual is one who remains calm and rational, regardless of external circumstances, embodying an inner peace that reflects true greatness.

Existentialist philosophers like Jean-Paul Sartre and Simone de Beauvoir offer a different perspective, focusing on the authenticity of individual choice and the creation of meaning in a seemingly indifferent universe. For existentialists, nobility is found in the courage to face the absurdity of existence and to forge one's own path with integrity and authenticity. Sartre's famous declaration, 'existence precedes essence', underscores the belief that individuals are free to define themselves through their actions. In this view, nobility involves a radical honesty with oneself and the world, taking full responsibility for one's choices and striving to live in a way that is true to one's deepest values.

Buddhist philosophy introduces the concept of nobility through the Four Noble Truths and the Eightfold Path, emphasizing the cultivation of compassion, mindfulness, and ethical living. The Buddha taught that true nobility lies in the alleviation of suffering, both for oneself and others. The *Dhammapada* says, 'The truly noble person is one who does no harm in the world.' Buddhist nobility is thus deeply connected to the practice of compassion (*karuna*) and loving-kindness (*metta*). It involves a commitment to understanding and mitigating the causes of suffering, embracing a way of life that promotes harmony, peace, and enlightenment.

At the heart of nobility lies character – the sum of virtues that defines an individual's essence. Integrity stands tall as a pillar of nobility, anchoring actions firmly in the bedrock of moral rectitude. A noble person walks the path of honesty and transparency, their words echoing the resonance of truth. Courage, another facet of noble character, unfurls its banner in the face of adversity, daring to stand firm against the tempests of life. Compassion, that gentle touch of humanity, softens the edges of the world's hardships. A noble soul extends a hand in empathy, embracing the pain of others as their own. Kindness flows forth like a river, nurturing parched hearts with its soothing balm. Generosity, too, finds its home within the chambers of nobility, as the noble spirit shares its blessings freely.

Nobility finds expression not only in character but also in action. It is in the selfless deeds that we witness the true measure of a noble heart. To serve others without thought of personal gain, to lift the downtrodden and shield the vulnerable – these are the hallmarks of noble conduct. In the quiet moments of everyday life, nobility finds its canvas. A kind word spoken to a stranger, a helping hand extended to a neighbour in need – these seemingly small gestures ripple outward, leaving an indelible mark on the fabric of human connection. It is in the grand gestures, too, that nobility shines brightly – a leader who sacrifices their own comfort for the welfare of their people, a philanthropist who dedicates their wealth to alleviate the suffering of others.

The Manifestation of Nobility in Modern Life

In a world dominated by technological advancements, rapid information exchange, and a globalized economy, the concept of nobility may seem archaic or relegated to the annals of history. Traditionally associated with hereditary titles, wealth, and a code of chivalry, nobility appears as a relic of the past. However, the essence of nobility transcends these historical confines and manifests in various forms in modern life. In today's context, nobility can be seen through the lens of moral excellence, selflessness, integrity, and leadership.

One of the contemporary manifestations of nobility is moral excellence and integrity. In an age where scandals and ethical breaches are frequently exposed in both public and private sectors, individuals who uphold strong moral principles are often revered. This form of nobility is not about flawless perfection but about the consistent effort to do what is right, even when it is difficult or unpopular. For instance, whistle-blowers like Edward Snowden and Frances Haugen have exemplified modern nobility. By exposing unethical practices and risking their careers and personal lives, they have demonstrated a commitment to truth and transparency, reflecting a deep sense of responsibility and courage, qualities traditionally associated with noble character.

Selflessness and altruism are other manifestations of nobility in the contemporary society. These qualities are evident in individuals and organizations dedicated to humanitarian causes, environmental conservation, and social justice. Take the example of Greta Thunberg's activism for climate change. Despite her young age, Thunberg's unwavering dedication to environmental advocacy has mobilized millions and brought urgent attention to climate issues. Her actions embody the noble spirit of sacrificing personal comfort for the greater good. Similarly, consider the work of Malala Yousafzai, who, despite facing life-threatening danger, advocates for girls' education globally, highlighting a selfless commitment to a cause greater than herself.

Leadership, when guided by a vision of positive change and ethical principles, is another key aspect of modern nobility. Leaders who prioritize the well-being of their followers and act with integrity and empathy are often seen as noble figures. Jacinda Ardern, the former Prime Minister of New Zealand, exemplifies this type of leadership. Her compassionate response to the Christchurch Mosque shootings and her decisive handling of the COVID-19 pandemic have been widely praised. Ardern's leadership style, marked by empathy, inclusiveness, and a commitment to justice, resonates with the noble qualities of traditional leadership adapted to contemporary challenges. In the business world, leaders like Satya Nadella of Microsoft have transformed corporate cultures by emphasizing empathy, collaboration, and ethical responsibility. Microsoft has not only achieved significant financial success, but has also become a more inclusive and socially responsible company.

Nobility also finds expression in the pursuit of knowledge and artistic excellence. Scholars, scientists, and artists who push the boundaries of human understanding and creativity often do so with little regard for financial gain or personal recognition. Their contributions enrich society and inspire future generations. The work of scientists like Dr Jennifer Doudna, a pioneer in CRISPR gene editing technology, showcases how intellectual pursuits can reflect noble aspirations. Her ground-breaking research holds the potential to revolutionize medicine and improve countless lives. As a prominent immunologist and a key figure in the response to the HIV/AIDS crisis and the COVID-19 pandemic, Dr Anthony Fauci's career reflects a lifetime commitment to public health. His dedication to advancing medical science and his unwavering efforts to communicate accurate information during crises demonstrate the noble qualities of integrity, resilience, and service to humanity.

While the actions of high-profile individuals are often highlighted, nobility is also evident in the everyday deeds of ordinary people. Acts of kindness, integrity, and selflessness contribute to the fabric of a noble society. During the COVID-19 pandemic, countless healthcare workers, grocery store employees, delivery drivers, and other essential workers displayed remarkable nobility. Despite the risks to their health and safety, they continued to perform their duties, often going above and beyond to ensure that society's needs were met. Their dedication and resilience highlighted the noble spirit of service and sacrifice in everyday life. In communities around the world, people volunteer their time and resources to help those in need. From organizing food drives to mentoring at-risk youth, these acts demonstrate how nobility can permeate daily life.

Cultivating Nobility

Cultivating nobility within oneself requires intentional effort and a genuine commitment to self-reflection and personal growth. It involves a deep exploration of one's values, principles, and actions, aiming to align them harmoniously. This alignment serves as the foundation upon which a noble character is built. Through introspection, individuals gain clarity on their core beliefs and assess how these values manifest in their daily actions and decisions, marking a crucial first step toward nurturing nobility within. Integral to this cultivation is an unwavering commitment to personal integrity. It involves being honest and authentic in both word and deed, fostering trust and respect in relationships with oneself and others. Compassion is another essential aspect of nurturing nobility. Cultivating empathy allows individuals to understand and connect with the experiences and emotions of those around them. By actively practicing compassion, individuals uplift and support others, contributing to the greater good of society and fostering a sense of interconnectedness.

Embracing lifelong learning is a hallmark of noble character. Continuously pursuing knowledge and wisdom expands one's understanding of the world and deepens one's capacity for empathy and compassion. Courage is indispensable on the path to nobility. It requires standing up for what is right, even in the face of adversity or opposition. Acting with courage means advocating for justice, challenging injustice, and taking risks to uphold one's principles and values, regardless of personal cost. Fostering a sense of community is also integral to cultivating nobility. Building and nurturing meaningful relationships that support mutual growth and well-being strengthens the fabric of society. By actively participating in community initiatives and supporting others, individuals contribute to the collective good, fostering a sense of belonging and interconnectedness.

The Japanese concept of '*ikigai*,' which means 'a reason for being,' encourages individuals to find joy and purpose in the small, everyday actions that contribute to the well-being of others and oneself. By aligning one's daily activities with a sense of purpose and ethical commitment, one can lead a noble life, regardless of the scale of their actions. Cultivating nobility through ikigai involves embracing a holistic approach to life that integrates personal fulfilment with a contribution to the greater good. Ikigai encourages individuals to seek out and nurture the intersections of what they love, what they are good at, what the world needs, and what they can be rewarded for. This framework not only emphasizes the importance of finding joy and meaning in one's daily activities but also underscores the significance of ethical commitment and consideration for others. By aligning one's daily activities with a sense of purpose and ethical commitment, individuals can cultivate nobility in their lives. Furthermore, ikigai encourages individuals to reflect on their values and priorities, leading to a deeper understanding of what truly matters to them. This introspection can guide decision-making processes and inspire actions that are in line with one's sense of purpose and ethical principles. In this way, ikigai serves as a compass for leading a noble life, guiding individuals towards actions that are not only fulfilling for themselves but also beneficial to the broader community.

Are you Noble?

Can an ordinary person be noble, or does nobility require extraordinary actions? The truth is, nobility is not confined to grand gestures or heroic feats. While history celebrates those who have performed extraordinary deeds, true nobility can be found in the everyday actions of ordinary people. You are noble if you prioritize the well-being of others over personal gain. A noble person acts out of a genuine desire to help and support those in need, regardless of the potential costs to themselves. This selflessness is a hallmark of true nobility. You are noble if you exhibit integrity and honesty in all your dealings. Noble deeds are grounded in truth and righteousness, avoiding deceit or manipulation. Upholding these principles, even when it is challenging, demonstrates a commitment to ethical conduct and earns the trust and respect of others. You are noble if you show empathy and compassion towards others. Understanding and sharing the feelings of others, especially during times of suffering or distress, is a key aspect of noble character.

Compassion drives you to take action to alleviate pain and bring comfort, embodying the spirit of kindness and humanity. You are noble if you have the courage to stand up for what is right, even in the face of adversity. Noble actions often require bravery, whether it is speaking out against injustice, protecting the vulnerable, or making sacrifices for a greater cause, inspiring others and creating a ripple effect of positive change. You are noble if you contribute to the greater good of your community and society. Whether through volunteer work, activism, or simply helping a neighbour, your actions reflect a dedication to improving the world around you. This commitment to the common good highlights the interconnectedness of humanity and the importance of collective effort. You are noble if you practise humility and recognize the value of every individual. Nobility is not about seeking praise or recognition but about serving others with humility and respect. A noble person values the dignity of all people and treats everyone with kindness and consideration. Noble deeds often require resilience and determination. Whether you are fighting for justice, helping during a crisis, or supporting someone through a difficult time, your perseverance demonstrates a steadfast commitment to making a positive impact.

'Society becomes better when old men plant trees in whose shade they know they will never sit.' This metaphorical planting of trees represents actions taken not for immediate benefit or personal gain but for the long-term well-being of others. Such deeds embody the highest form of nobility and provide a powerful model for fostering a compassionate and thriving society. When individuals engage in actions that benefit future generations, they demonstrate a level of selflessness and forward-thinking that transcends personal or immediate concerns. It highlights the importance of considering the long-term consequences of our actions and ensuring that our efforts contribute to the greater good. This perspective is crucial for addressing some of the most pressing issues facing humanity today, such as environmental sustainability, social justice, and global health. By adopting a mind-set that prioritizes the welfare of future generations, we can make more thoughtful and impactful decisions that promote lasting positive change. Generosity can be found in everyday acts of kindness, such as volunteering time to help others, donating resources to those in need, or simply offering a kind word or gesture. These small acts, when accumulated, significantly enhance the social fabric and overall well-being of communities. Planting trees symbolizes the creation of a legacy that extends beyond one's lifetime. This legacy is built on the principles of service, compassion, and stewardship. By engaging in noble deeds, individuals leave behind a world that is better for them having been in it. This legacy is not measured by personal accolades or material wealth but by the positive impact one has on others and on society as a whole. It serves as a reminder that true fulfilment and purpose are found in serving others and contributing to the greater good. This enduring influence helps to shape the values and behaviour of future generations, promoting a cycle of continuous improvement and compassion. Hope and optimism are contagious. When individuals see others taking steps to improve the future, it reinforces their own belief in the possibility of positive change and encourages them to contribute to these efforts. This collective optimism can drive significant progress and innovation, helping to address complex social and environmental issues.

***

Chapter 13

Being Human

The greatness of humanity is not in being human, but in being humane

—Mahatma Gandhi

What does it mean to be human? To ponder the essence of humanity is to dig into the very core of our existence. At the heart of being human lies our consciousness, a complex and extraordinary phenomenon that sets us apart from other living beings. Human consciousness embraces not only our awareness of the world around us but also our self-awareness – the profound ability to reflect on our own thoughts, emotions, and experiences. This self-reflective capacity allows us to ask fundamental questions about our existence: Who am I? Why am I here? What is my purpose? Such introspection is unique to humans and forms the bedrock of our intellectual and spiritual lives. Self-awareness also brings with it a sense of individuality. This sense of individuality fosters a personal narrative – a story we tell ourselves about who we are, where we come from, and where we are going. Self-awareness allows us to experience complex emotions such as guilt, pride, and empathy.

Another profound aspect of human existence is our awareness of mortality. Unlike other species, humans possess an acute awareness of their own finitude. The knowledge that our lives are limited in time impels us to seek meaning and purpose.

This awareness of death casts a shadow over our existence but also illuminates it, giving urgency and significance to our actions. The quest for meaning in the face of mortality is a central theme in many philosophical and religious traditions. Some find solace in the belief in an afterlife or a higher power, while others seek meaning through personal achievements, relationships, or contributions to society. Regardless of the path taken, the search for meaning is a fundamental aspect of the human condition. This existential quest can lead to profound insights and personal growth. It encourages us to reflect on what truly matters, to prioritize our values, and to live authentically. The recognition of our mortality can also inspire us to make the most of our time, to embrace life's fleeting moments, and to appreciate the beauty and fragility of existence.

Consciousness is perhaps the most mysterious and fascinating aspect of being human. It is the state of being aware of and able to think about one's own existence, sensations, thoughts, and surroundings. This self-reflective consciousness enables humans to create, innovate, and imagine possibilities beyond immediate reality. Creativity is a direct manifestation of human consciousness. It allows us to transform our thoughts and emotions into tangible expressions, whether through art, music, literature, or scientific discovery. Creativity is also a way of connecting with others and contributing to the collective human experience. The ability to imagine and create has led to the development of complex cultures and civilizations. It has enabled us to build societies, develop technologies, and explore the universe. Creativity is a testament to the boundless potential of the human mind.

Human beings possess a distinct ethical and moral consciousness. We have the ability to discern right from wrong, to reflect on the consequences of our actions, and to make choices based on ethical principles. Moral consciousness is not only an individual trait but also a collective one. Societies develop moral codes and ethical frameworks that guide behaviour and promote social harmony. These moral systems are often influenced by cultural, religious, and philosophical traditions. It reflects the diverse ways in which humans seek to live meaningful and just lives. Ethical reflection is an ongoing process. It involves questioning our assumptions. This moral striving is a key aspect of what it means to be human. It drives us to seek justice, compassion, and integrity in our interactions with others.

Language is another defining feature of humanity. It is through language that we communicate our thoughts, share our experiences, and pass down knowledge across generations. Language allows us to connect with others, to collaborate, and to build complex social structures. The development of language has been a crucial factor in the evolution of human societies. It has enabled us to share ideas, express emotions, and record our history. Language is not only a tool for communication but also a medium for self-expression and cultural identity. Through language, we create stories, myths, and legends that convey the values and beliefs of our communities. Language is a powerful force that unites us, enriches our lives, and allows us to transcend the limitations of our individual existence.

Being human involves recognizing our interconnectedness with all forms of life. While self-awareness and individuality are central to our experience, we are also part of a larger web of existence. This interconnectedness is evident in our relationships with other people, with nature, and with the universe as a whole. Understanding our place in this web fosters a sense of responsibility and stewardship. It encourages us to consider the impact of our actions on the environment, on other species, and on future generations. This holistic perspective can lead to a deeper appreciation of the interconnectedness of life and a commitment to living in harmony with the world around us.

Spectrum of Human Emotions

Emotions are the vibrant colours of the human experience, painting our lives with shades of joy, sorrow, love, and anger. These feelings are fundamental to our humanity, shaping our perceptions, guiding our actions, and enriching our interactions. Unlike mere responses to external stimuli, emotions are integral components of our inner world. It influences our thoughts, decisions, and behaviours. Joy, for instance, can emerge from simple pleasures such as the warmth of the sun, the taste of a favourite food, or the laughter of a loved one. It can also spring from deeper sources like achieving a personal goal, experiencing love, or feeling a sense of purpose. Happiness, as a sustained state of joy, is often seen as a primary goal in life, with many philosophical, psychological, and spiritual traditions exploring how to attain it. Gratitude, mindfulness, and meaningful connections are frequently highlighted as paths to true happiness. Yet, sorrow is an inevitable part of the human condition, arising from loss, disappointment, or unfulfilled desires. Grief, the intense sorrow following a significant loss, such as the death of a loved one, can be overwhelming. These emotions remind us of the transient nature of life.

However, they also offer opportunities for growth and empathy. Through sorrow and grief, we can gain a deeper understanding of ourselves and others. Love, in its many forms – romantic, familial, and platonic – is a complex and multifaceted emotion characterized by deep affection, attachment, and care for another person. It motivates us to form connections, build relationships, and nurture those we care about. Affection, a milder form of love, manifests in gestures of warmth and fondness. It contributes to our emotional well-being and sense of belonging. Anger, a natural response to perceived threats, injustices, or frustrations, is often viewed negatively. However, it can also be a catalyst for change, which prompts us to address wrongs and seek justice. Fear is another protective emotion. Anxiety, a prolonged state of fear or worry, can arise from uncertainties about the future or perceived threats. While fear can be lifesaving, excessive anxiety can impair our ability to function and enjoy life.

Empathy is the ability to understand and share the feelings of others. It is the bridge that connects us which enables us to form deep and meaningful relationships. Empathy involves both cognitive and emotional components: the ability to intellectually grasp another person's perspective and to emotionally resonate with their feelings. Neuroscientific research has identified mirror neurons, specialized brain cells that activate both when we perform an action and when we observe someone else performing the same action. When we see someone in pain, our mirror neurons fire in a way that enables us to feel a semblance of their suffering, fostering compassion and a desire to help. Empathy is fundamental to the formation and maintenance of social bonds. In families, empathy helps parents understand and respond to their children's needs, and strengthens the parent-child bond. In friendships, empathy allows us to share joys and sorrows. In romantic relationships, empathy is essential for understanding and meeting each other's emotional needs. Often, empathy motivates altruistic behaviour – the selfless concern for the well-being of others. When we empathize with someone's suffering, we are moved to alleviate their distress, even at a personal cost. This altruistic impulse is evident in acts of kindness, charity, and volunteerism. Empathy-driven altruism contributes to social harmony and collective well-being, creating a more compassionate and just society. Compassion is empathy in action. It is the heartfelt desire to alleviate the suffering of others and promote their well-being. Compassion goes beyond mere understanding; it involves a commitment to take steps to reduce pain and enhance happiness. Research in psychology and neuroscience has shown that compassion has positive effects on both the giver and the receiver. Compassionate individuals tend to experience greater emotional well-being, lower stress levels, and enhanced social connections. Practicing compassion activates reward centres in the brain, releasing feel-good neurotransmitters like oxytocin, which promote feelings of happiness and bonding.

Emotions play a critical role in decision making, influencing our choices and actions in profound ways and making us more human. While rational thought is essential for weighing options and considering consequences, emotions provide valuable information about our values, priorities, and needs. They act as internal signals, guiding us toward decisions that align with our deeper motivations and well-being. Emotional intelligence (EI), the ability to recognize, understand, and manage our own emotions and the emotions of others, is associated with better decision-making skills. High EI enables us to navigate complex emotional landscapes, resolve conflicts, and build strong relationships. The somatic marker hypothesis, proposed by neuroscientist Antonio Damasio, suggests that emotions are crucial for making sound decisions. According to this hypothesis, emotional experiences leave 'markers' in the brain that influence future decision-making. These markers, associated with positive or negative outcomes, guide us in evaluating options. For example, a gut feeling or intuitive response can serve as a somatic marker, alerting us to potential risks or benefits that may not be immediately apparent through rational analysis alone.

The Quest for Meaning and Purpose

Human existence is marked by a quest for meaning and purpose. This quest is a driving force behind much of our intellectual, spiritual, and emotional endeavours. It shapes our lives, influences our decisions, and gives us a sense of direction. Unlike other species, humans possess a unique awareness of their own finitude, a consciousness of mortality that propels us to seek out reasons for our existence. This awareness of death casts a shadow over our lives but also illuminates it, infusing our actions with urgency and significance. From the earliest days of human history, people have sought to understand their place in the cosmos. Ancient myths and legends, religious doctrines, and philosophical systems have all attempted to provide an answer to the fundamental question of life: What is the purpose of our existence? This has led to the creation of complex belief systems and cultural narratives.

Religion has a central role in the human quest for meaning. Across cultures and epochs, religious beliefs have provided explanations for the mysteries of existence, offering narratives that connect individual lives to a greater cosmic order. Religions propose that life has intrinsic value and purpose, often defined by adherence to divine laws, pursuit of spiritual enlightenment, or preparation for an afterlife. These beliefs offer comfort in the face of life's uncertainties and losses. In addition to religious frameworks, philosophy has been a vital opportunity for exploring meaning and purpose. Philosophers from Socrates to Sartre have grappled with existential questions, examining the nature of reality, the self, and the moral imperatives that govern our actions. Existentialist thinkers, for example, emphasize personal responsibility and the freedom to create meaning through individual choices. They argue that in a world devoid of inherent meaning, humans must construct their own purposes through authentic engagement with life.

For many, the search for meaning is closely tied to personal achievements and aspirations. This secular perspective emphasizes self-actualization and the fulfilment of potential. Psychologist Abraham Maslow's hierarchy of needs outlines a progression from basic survival needs to higher-order pursuits such as esteem and self-actualization. According to Maslow, once our fundamental needs for safety, love, and belonging are met, we are motivated to seek personal growth, creativity, and self-fulfilment. Achieving one's potential, whether through career success, artistic expression, or personal development, becomes a significant source of meaning.

Relationships also play a central role in our quest for purpose. Humans are inherently social beings, and our connections with others provide a profound sense of meaning and fulfilment. Love, friendship, and family relationships offer support, understanding, and a sense of continuity. These bonds remind us that we are part of something larger than ourselves, a network of interdependent lives that shape and are shaped by our actions. Through nurturing relationships, we find purpose.

The pursuit of meaning often extends beyond individual fulfilment to encompass contributions to the broader community and the world. Altruistic endeavours, such as volunteering, activism, and social work, reflect a desire to make a positive impact and leave the world better than we found it. Engaging in these activities can provide a deep sense of purpose, as we align our actions with values such as justice, compassion, and service.

Human life is punctuated by moments of adversity – challenges and hardships that test our resolve and shape our character. These trials are not merely obstacles to overcome, but integral to our personal growth and resilience. Adversity forces us to confront our limitations, adapt to unforeseen circumstances, and discover untapped reservoirs of strength. Each challenge presents an opportunity for learning and transformation, fostering resilience that equips us to face future obstacles with greater fortitude and wisdom. Throughout history and literature, stories abound of individuals who have triumphed over adversity. These narratives resonate because they embody the human capacity for hope and perseverance in the face of seemingly insurmountable odds. From ancient epics to modern-day accounts, tales of resilience inspire and uplift, demonstrating the indomitable spirit that drives us to persevere in pursuit of our goals and ideals. These stories remind us that adversity, while daunting, can be a catalyst for growth, pushing us beyond our comfort zones and catalysing personal development. Hope is a beacon that guides us through the darkest of times, infusing our struggles with purpose and meaning. The human capacity for hope transcends individual circumstances, offering solace and motivation to persevere in the face of uncertainty. Perseverance complements hope, embodying steadfast commitment. It is the willingness to persist in the face of setbacks.

In the modern era, the quest for meaning has also taken on new dimensions with the rise of science and technology. Scientific inquiry, driven by curiosity and a desire to understand the natural world, offers insights into the mysteries of existence. The discoveries of cosmology, biology, and physics reveal the intricate workings of the universe and our place within it. The technological revolution, with its innovations in communication, medicine, and artificial intelligence, also raises ethical questions about the future of humanity and the responsibilities that come with our expanding capabilities. The recognition of our interconnectedness with all forms of life further enriches our quest for meaning. As we become more aware of the ecological and ethical implications of our actions, a sense of stewardship emerges. Understanding our place within the broader web of life fosters a sense of responsibility to protect and preserve the environment. This ecological consciousness can inspire purposeful actions aimed at sustainability, conservation, and the harmonious coexistence of all species.

Social Beings

We have already explored how humans are fundamentally social beings, distinguished by their intricate and evolving systems of societal organization. From the earliest tribes to modern global communities, our strong sense of society has been a defining characteristic that shapes almost every aspect of human life. The roots of human societal organization can be traced back to our early ancestors who lived in small bands or tribes. These groups provided safety, support, and shared resources, essential for survival in challenging environments. Early humans relied on collaboration and division of labour to hunt, gather food, and protect against predators. This cooperative behaviour laid the foundation for complex social structures and cultural norms that continue to evolve today.

As human societies transitioned from nomadic lifestyles to settled agricultural communities, permanent settlements emerged, fostering more stable social structures. Agriculture enabled the development of surplus food production, leading to specialization in crafts, trade, and governance. This specialization gave rise to hierarchical systems of authority and labour, as well as the emergence of early forms of governance and societal roles.

Over millennia, human societies have evolved diverse forms of social organization, shaped by geography, ecology, technology, and cultural practices. From ancient civilizations like Mesopotamia, Egypt, and China to classical societies in Greece and Rome, each era produced distinct social hierarchies, legal codes, and cultural achievements. These societies were characterized by complex networks of relationships, institutions, and shared beliefs that governed behaviour and shaped individual identities. Religious and philosophical traditions have also played a crucial role in shaping societal values and norms. Moral teachings and ethical principles articulated by religious leaders and thinkers have guided social behaviour, reinforced community bonds, and provided frameworks for justice and governance. These belief systems continue to influence societal norms, ethical dilemmas, and individual conduct in contemporary societies.

Human societies rely on institutions – formal and informal organizations – to structure social interactions, regulate behaviour, and address collective needs. Institutions such as government, education, healthcare, and religious organizations play vital roles in maintaining social order, promoting justice, and providing essential services. Governance systems, ranging from democratic to authoritarian, reflect varying approaches to decision-making, representation, and accountability within societies. Law and justice systems establish legal frameworks that define rights, responsibilities, and consequences for behaviour. Legal codes evolve in response to societal changes and ethical considerations, aiming to uphold fairness, protect individual liberties, and promote social harmony. The rule of law, upheld by impartial courts and legal institutions, serves as a cornerstone of democratic governance.

Economic systems shape societal organization by determining how resources are produced, distributed, and consumed within communities. From subsistence economies based on hunting and gathering to modern global markets driven by technology and finance, economic systems influence social mobility, inequality, and access to opportunities. Trade networks, dating back to ancient times, facilitated cultural exchange, technological innovation, and economic prosperity, linking distant societies and fostering intercultural understanding. Labour markets and employment opportunities are integral to economic systems, providing individuals with means to support themselves and contribute to society. Technological advancements, such as industrialization and digitalization, have transformed economic landscapes, creating new industries, jobs, and economic disparities. Social policies and welfare programmes seek to address economic inequalities and promote social mobility.

Social cohesion refers to the degree of solidarity and mutual support within communities, fostering trust, cooperation, and a sense of shared purpose. Strong social cohesion promotes resilience during times of crisis, encourages civic engagement, and enhances collective well-being. Collective identity emerges from shared experiences, values, and symbols that unify individuals within a society or community. National identity, for example, encompasses a shared sense of belonging and loyalty to a nation-state, often defined by common history, language, traditions, and citizenship. Collective identities can also be based on ethnicity, religion, gender, or shared interests, providing individuals with a sense of belonging and solidarity within diverse social contexts.

Legacy: Shaping the World for Future Generations

Human existence is marked by an awareness of time and a desire to leave a lasting imprint on the world. This aspiration to create a meaningful legacy reflects our innate sense of purpose and the recognition that our actions and contributions can shape the course of history for future generations. Our legacy encompasses not only tangible achievements but also the values, ideals, and cultural heritage we pass on to those who come after us. At its core, legacy is the enduring impact of our lives – the imprint we leave on individuals, communities, and the world at large. It is shaped by our actions, decisions, and interactions with others, reflecting our values, passions, and aspirations. While legacy is often associated with notable achievements or historical milestones, it also encompasses everyday acts of kindness, wisdom shared with loved ones, and the values we instil in future generations. The choices we make today – from environmental stewardship to technological innovation – have far-reaching consequences that shape the world our descendants will inherit.

Our collective impact on climate change, biodiversity, and global health underscores the intergenerational responsibility to safeguard the planet and ensure its sustainability for future inhabitants. Similarly, advancements in science, medicine, and technology have the potential to revolutionize industries, enhance quality of life, and expand opportunities for future generations. Cultural and artistic legacies play a vital role in preserving and transmitting knowledge, traditions, and creative expressions across time. Literature, music, visual arts, and oral traditions serve as repositories of human experiences and collective wisdom.

History provides insights into the impact of individuals and societies on shaping the course of human events. From visionary leaders and social reformers to grassroots movements and scientific breakthroughs, historical legacies illustrate the transformative power of collective action. The legacies of figures like Mahatma Gandhi, Martin Luther King Jr, Marie Curie, and Nelson Mandela inspire future generations to advocate for justice, pursue knowledge, and champion causes that advance human flourishing and global peace. Individually, our personal and professional pursuits contribute to our legacy by reflecting our unique talents, values, and achievements. Whether through career accomplishments, philanthropic endeavours, or family traditions, our actions leave an indelible mark on those around us and shape the narratives that define our lives. Mentorship, education, and community engagement offer opportunities to empower others, impart knowledge, and cultivate leadership skills that endure beyond our lifetimes.

Our capacity to contemplate and intentionally shape our legacy sets humans apart from other species in intense ways. While many animals exhibit complex social behaviours and even forms of cultural transmission, the depth and breadth of human legacy-making are uniquely human attributes that distinguish us. Humans possess a remarkable ability for conscious reflection on the past, present, and future. Unlike instinct-driven behaviours seen in many animals, our decisions are often guided by deliberation and foresight. We not only react to immediate stimuli but also consider long-term consequences and aspire to leave a meaningful impact on future generations.

Human societies excel in the transmission of cultural knowledge and practices across generations. Through language, storytelling, art, and education, we pass down accumulated wisdom, values, and traditions that define our identities and shape our interactions. This collective learning enables us to build upon the achievements of our predecessors, advancing knowledge and technology at an exponential rate compared to other species. Our ability to innovate and adapt cultural practices also contributes to our resilience and capacity to thrive in diverse environments. The development of symbolic thinking and artistic expression is another hallmark of human distinctiveness. Through language, symbols, and artistic forms such as painting, music, and literature, we communicate abstract concepts, emotions, and experiences.

Art serves not only as a means of creative expression but also as a vehicle for cultural preservation, social commentary, and collective memory. The ability to create and appreciate art reflects our capacity for introspection, imagination, and empathy. Unlike many species that operate on short-term survival instincts, humans engage in long-term planning and goal pursuit. This forward-thinking mentality is evident in our agricultural practices, urban planning, scientific research, and economic strategies. From building infrastructure to mitigating environmental impacts, our ability to envision future outcomes, and work collectively toward shared objectives demonstrates a capacity for complex problem-solving and collaboration on a global scale.

***

Chapter 14

Who Enjoys Life?

The purpose of life is to live it, to taste experience to the utmost, to reach out eagerly and without fear for newer and richer experience.

—Eleanor Roosevelt

Enjoyment is a state of mind that transcends mere pleasure. It is the deep-seated contentment and satisfaction derived from engaging with life in a meaningful way. Unlike fleeting pleasures that offer momentary gratification, true enjoyment encompasses a holistic sense of well-being and fulfilment. It is about appreciating the present moment, finding beauty in the mundane, and connecting deeply with our surroundings and ourselves. To truly enjoy life, one must cultivate a mind-set that embraces the present. Such a state of presence is where joy flourishes, unhindered by the distractions and pressures of modern life. It is about being aware of the simple pleasures – the warmth of the sun on your skin, the aroma of fresh coffee, the laughter of a loved one – and recognizing these moments as precious. True enjoyment is intrinsically linked to a sense of purpose. It arises when we align our actions with our values and passions, creating a life that feels authentic and meaningful.

Cultural context plays a significant role in shaping how people perceive and practice enjoyment. Different cultures offer unique insights and approaches to living a joyful life, often reflecting their historical, social, and philosophical backgrounds. In Western cultures, particularly in the United States, enjoyment is often associated with the pursuit of happiness. This pursuit is seen as an individual right, deeply embedded in the cultural ethos, as epitomized by the Declaration of Independence. The American Dream itself is a testament to this belief, where happiness is pursued through success, wealth, and personal freedom. Enjoyment, in this context, is often linked to personal achievements and material abundance.

In contrast, many Eastern cultures, such as those in China and Japan, emphasize harmony and balance as pathways to enjoyment. The Chinese concept of *'Chi'* and the Japanese principle of *'Ikigai'* reflect a holistic approach to life. Chi refers to the vital life force that flows through all living things, and maintaining its balance leads to health and happiness. Ikigai, on the other hand, is about finding joy in life through a sense of purpose and dedication to something greater than oneself. These concepts encourage living a balanced life, where joy is found in everyday activities and communal harmony. Scandinavian cultures, renowned for their high quality of life, offer the concept of '*hygge*' (Denmark) and '*lagom*' (Sweden). Hygge focuses on creating a warm, cozy environment and enjoying the simple pleasures of life, such as spending time with loved ones, indulging in comfort foods, and appreciating the present moment. Lagom advocates for moderation and balance, suggesting that enjoyment comes from not too little, not too much, but just the right amount of everything. In Latin American cultures, the concept of *'alegría'* or joy is often expressed through vibrant social interactions, music, dance, and festivals. The communal aspect of enjoyment is significant here, where joy is amplified through shared experiences and collective celebrations.

Philosophers throughout history have pondered the nature of joy and contentment, offering profound insights that continue to resonate today. In Eastern philosophy, the teachings of Laozi and the principles of Taoism highlight the importance of living in harmony with the Tao, or the natural way of the universe. Taoism advocates for simplicity, spontaneity, and non-striving, suggesting that true enjoyment comes from aligning oneself with the natural flow of life and letting go of excessive desires and ambitions. The Buddhist concept of '*ananda*', meaning bliss, suggests that true joy arises from a deep state of inner peace and enlightenment. Buddhism teaches that by letting go of attachments and desires, one can achieve a state of Nirvana, where suffering ceases and true bliss is experienced. This perspective highlights the importance of mindfulness, meditation, and inner tranquility in cultivating joy.

Modern philosophers also contribute to our understanding of enjoyment. Existentialist thinkers like Jean-Paul Sartre and Albert Camus explore the idea of finding meaning and joy in an inherently meaningless world. They suggest that individuals must create their own meaning and embrace the freedom and responsibility that comes with it. This existential joy is about living authentically and fully embracing the human condition. In contemporary philosophy, positive psychology, spearheaded by figures like Martin Seligman, emphasizes the scientific study of happiness and well-being. Seligman's PERMA model (Positive Emotion, Engagement, Relationships, Meaning, and Accomplishment) provides a framework for understanding the components of a fulfilling life. According to this model, true enjoyment comprises positive emotions, deep engagement in activities, meaningful relationships, a sense of purpose, and the achievement of goals.

The Social Dimension of Joy

At the heart of human joy lies the intricate mesh of relationships and connections that we form throughout our lives. Meaningful relationships serve as a foundation for our well-being, providing emotional support, shared experiences, and a sense of belonging. The significance of these connections cannot be overstated, as they deeply impact our happiness and overall life satisfaction. Human beings are inherently social creatures. From the moment we are born, we rely on others for survival, learning, and emotional development. This intrinsic need for connection continues throughout our lives. Research consistently shows that individuals with strong, supportive relationships tend to be happier, healthier, and live longer. Meaningful relationships provide a safe space for individuals to express their thoughts, feelings, and vulnerabilities. They offer emotional support during times of stress and adversity, acting as a buffer against the challenges of life. The presence of a trusted friend or loved one can significantly reduce feelings of loneliness and isolation, fostering a sense of security and belonging. Furthermore, relationships enrich our lives through shared experiences and mutual growth. Whether it's the joy of celebrating milestones, the comfort of shared memories, or the satisfaction of mutual achievements, these connections add depth and richness to our lives. Romantic relationships, in particular, play a unique role in our happiness. The deep emotional and physical intimacy shared with a partner can be a profound source of joy and fulfilment. Similarly, family bonds, often characterized by unconditional love and support, provide a foundation of stability and continuity. Friendships, too, are vital. Friends offer companionship, laughter, and shared interests, creating a sense of community and mutual support. Authentic, deep connections foster a sense of being understood and valued.

The feeling of belonging to a community and contributing to its well-being is an aspect of the social dimension of joy. Communities provide a sense of identity and purpose, offering a collective sense of belonging that transcends individual experiences. Being part of a community fulfils our innate need for connection and acceptance. Whether it is a neighbourhood, a cultural or religious group, a professional network, or an interest-based club, communities offer a space where individuals can come together, share common values, and work towards shared goals. This collective identity fosters a sense of pride and solidarity. Communities also offer numerous opportunities for social interaction and engagement. Festivals, gatherings, and communal activities create spaces for people to come together, celebrate, and enjoy each other's company. These shared experiences strengthen social bonds and create lasting memories. The act of contributing to a community provides a deep sense of purpose and satisfaction. Whether it's through volunteering, participating in local events, or offering support to neighbours, giving back to the community enhances our sense of worth and belonging.

The joy derived from community involvement also buds from the social support and resources that communities provide. In times of need, communities often come together to offer assistance, whether through formal support systems or informal networks of care. This collective resilience creates a safety net. In essence, communities create a framework within which individuals can connect, support each other, and thrive. The joy of belonging to a community and contributing to its well-being is a testament to the power of collective human experience.

Acts of kindness and generosity are powerful catalysts for joy, benefiting both the giver and the receiver. Sharing resources, time, and compassion fosters a sense of interconnectedness and mutual support, enhancing our overall sense of happiness and well-being. Generosity is an expression of empathy and compassion. It involves recognizing the needs of others and responding with kindness and support. Whether it is through donating to charity, helping a friend in need, or offering a listening ear, acts of generosity create a ripple effect of positivity and connection. Generosity fosters social connections and strengthens relationships. Acts of kindness create bonds of trust and reciprocity. When we give generously, we often receive gratitude and appreciation in return. Studies have shown that individuals who engage in acts of kindness and charitable giving report higher levels of life satisfaction and emotional well-being. The 'helper's high', a term coined to describe the euphoric feeling experienced after helping others.

The Pursuit of Passion

To enjoy life fully, one must embark on the journey of discovering their passions. To uncover what truly excites and motivates us is to engage in a journey of self-discovery, a philosophical expedition into the depths of our soul. Passions are not always apparent; they often lie dormant, waiting to be awakened through introspection and reflection. We must dig into the archives of our experiences, seeking those moments where time seemed to dissolve, and our actions were driven by an intrinsic joy. These are the clues to our passions, hidden within the labyrinth of our memories and emotions. The process of identifying passions is akin to peeling back the layers of our constructed selves, revealing the core of our being. It requires a quieting of the external noise and a turning inward, a dialogue with our inner voice that often goes unheard in the cacophony of daily life. This inner dialogue is a philosophical practice, a Socratic method of questioning and uncovering truths that are uniquely ours. It is through exploration and experimentation that we encounter new facets of ourselves, often stumbling upon passions serendipitously. In this sense, life itself becomes a canvas, and we, the artists, discovering the colours that resonate most deeply with our soul.

The philosophical art of balancing passion and practicality is a delicate dance, one that requires wisdom and discernment. It is a recognition of the dual nature of our existence, where our higher aspirations must coexist with the mundane demands of daily life. Passion, in its purest form, is a pursuit of the soul, an expression of our deepest desires and creative energies. Yet, we inhabit a world bound by practicalities, where responsibilities and obligations cannot be ignored. The challenge lies in integrating our passions into this reality, creating a harmonious existence where both can thrive. It is to recognize that our passions need not be sacrificed at the altar of practicality, nor should our responsibilities be neglected in the pursuit of passion. Instead, it is about finding the intersections where they can coexist and enrich each other. This balance requires a mindful approach, where we allocate time and energy to our passions while honouring our commitments. It is a practice of setting priorities, where we discern what is essential and what can be adjusted. This discernment is not a one-time act but an ongoing process, a continual recalibration as we navigate the ebb and flow of life.

Mind-Set Matters

Those who think they are happy, are happy. This simple yet reflective observation highlights the transformative power of a positive mind-set. Our perception shapes our reality; therefore, cultivating a mind-set rooted in positivity is crucial for experiencing true enjoyment in life. Cultivating a joyful mind-set begins with the power of positive thinking and optimism. A positive mind-set significantly influences our ability to enjoy life. This perspective shapes our experiences and allows us to find joy even in the most challenging circumstances. Positive thinking is more than mere wishful thinking; it is a deliberate practice of focusing on the good, cultivating gratitude, and maintaining hope. Philosophically, this aligns with the principles of Stoicism, where the emphasis is placed on controlling our perceptions and reactions rather than external events. The Stoics believed that by adjusting our mind-set, we could transform our experience of the world, finding peace and contentment, regardless of our circumstances. Optimism, a forward-looking form of positive thinking, involves expecting good things to happen and seeing the potential for positive outcomes. This mind-set does not ignore the difficulties of life but rather acknowledges them while maintaining hope and confidence. Optimism fosters resilience and encourages us to take proactive steps towards our goals.

The impact of a positive mind-set on enjoyment is multidimensional. Positive thinkers are more likely to engage fully with life, savouring experiences and finding meaning in everyday moments. This approach enhances our emotional well-being, reduces stress, and improves our physical health. Research in positive psychology supports these claims, showing that optimism is linked to increased life satisfaction, better coping mechanisms, and greater overall happiness. A positive mind-set also influences our relationships and interactions with others. Optimistic individuals tend to be more approachable, empathetic, and supportive, fostering deeper connections and a sense of community.

Resilience and adaptability are essential components of a joyful mind-set. Resilience is the capacity to recover from setbacks, while adaptability is the ability to adjust to changing circumstances. Together, they form the foundation of a mind-set that can find joy even in adversity. Resilience involves cultivating a sense of inner strength, self-efficacy, and purpose. The philosophy of existentialism, with its focus on finding meaning in the face of life's inherent difficulties. Existentialist thinkers like Viktor Frankl emphasized the importance of finding purpose in suffering, suggesting that our response to adversity can be a source of profound personal growth and fulfilment. To build resilience, we must develop a mind-set that embraces challenges as opportunities for learning and growth. This involves fostering a growth mind-set, as proposed by psychologist Carol Dweck, which views abilities and intelligence as malleable rather than fixed. A growth mind-set encourages us to see failures as stepping stones to success and to persist in the face of obstacles. Adaptability complements resilience by enabling us to adjust our strategies and expectations in response to changing circumstances. This flexibility is crucial for maintaining a sense of joy and purpose when life does not go as planned.

Philosophically, the concept of impermanence in Buddhism teaches us to accept change as an integral part of life. Practically, building resilience and adaptability involves cultivating emotional regulation, problem-solving skills, and social support networks. Techniques such as mindfulness, cognitive-behavioural strategies, and stress management practices can enhance our ability to cope with adversity.

A joyful mind-set entails the principle of living authentically. Authenticity involves being true to oneself, aligning our actions and choices with our deepest values, beliefs, and desires. It is a commitment to living a life that reflects our true self, free from the constraints of external expectations and societal pressures. Philosophically, authenticity has been a central theme in existentialism and humanistic psychology. Living authentically requires self-awareness and self-acceptance. It involves an ongoing process of introspection, where we examine our values, passions, and aspirations. Authenticity also involves embracing our imperfections and vulnerabilities. By accepting and owning our imperfections, we can engage with the world more genuinely and connect with others on a deeper level. This vulnerability, as Brené Brown suggests, is the birthplace of joy, creativity, and meaningful relationships. Living authentically often requires courage, as it may involve challenging societal norms, risking disapproval, and stepping into the unknown. However, the rewards are immense. An authentic life is rich with purpose, meaning, and fulfilment. It allows us to pursue our passions wholeheartedly and to build relationships based on mutual respect and understanding.

Ultimately, joy is indeed extremely subjective. The subjective nature of joy becomes apparent when considering its triggers. What brings joy to one person may not necessarily evoke the same response in another. For some, joy arises from achieving personal milestones – whether academic, professional, or creative. It could be the exhilaration of mastering a skill, completing a project, or receiving recognition for one's efforts. These moments of accomplishment create a sense of pride and satisfaction that fuels joy. Conversely, joy can also emerge from simpler, more mundane experiences. It might be found in the laughter of loved ones, the warmth of a shared meal, or the serenity of a quiet moment spent in nature. These instances remind us that joy is often intertwined with our connections to others and the world around us.

***

Chapter 15

The Materialistic Happiness Paradox

He who is not contented with what he has, would not be contented with what he would like to have

—Socrates

Happiness, a term universally sought yet diversely defined, represents a state of well-being. In the contemporary world, especially in Western societies, happiness is often equated with material success – possessions, wealth, and status. This modern perception stands in contrast to many historical and cultural interpretations that emphasize inner peace and balance over external wealth. From a psychological perspective, happiness comprises both immediate pleasure and long-term fulfilment. It is a multi-dimensional construct involving emotional well-being, life satisfaction, and a sense of purpose. However, in today's consumer-driven culture, there is a strong inclination to associate happiness with material possessions. Advertisements, social media, and societal norms perpetuate the idea that acquiring more goods leads to a happier life, and many people equate their self-worth and success with the quantity and quality of their possessions.

This all started with the Industrial Revolution, which marked a significant shift in how happiness was perceived and pursued. The rapid advancements in technology and production led to unprecedented economic growth and the rise of consumer culture. For the first time in history, large segments of the population had access to goods and services that were previously unattainable. This newfound abundance fuelled the belief that material possessions were the key to happiness. Consumerism, a social and economic order that encourages the acquisition of goods and services in ever-increasing amounts, became a dominant force in Western societies. Advertising led to this transformation and created desires and aspirations for material goods. Companies and marketers began to associate products with happiness, success, and social status. The message was clear: to be happy, one needed to buy more and have more. This materialistic turn had deep implications for individual and collective conceptions of happiness. The focus shifted from inner fulfilment and ethical living to external wealth and consumption. Material possessions became symbols of success and happiness, which leaded to a culture of accumulation and excess. The more one had, the happier one was presumed to be.

However, this materialistic pursuit of happiness is fraught with problems. Psychological research has shown that while material wealth can improve well-being to a certain extent, its impact diminishes beyond a basic level of comfort and security. This phenomenon, known as the diminishing marginal utility of income, suggests that once basic needs are met, additional wealth has a limited effect on overall happiness. Yet, the societal pressure to accumulate more persists, often leading to stress, anxiety, and a perpetual sense of inadequacy. Materialism also impacts societal values and priorities. As material success becomes a primary goal, other important aspects of life, such as relationships, personal growth, and community involvement, may be neglected.

The Hedonic Treadmill

Material possessions often provide a sense of temporary satisfaction. This is rooted in the human tendency to experience pleasure and excitement when acquiring new items. Whether it's a new gadget, car, or piece of clothing, the initial acquisition brings a rush of happiness. However, this joy is typically short-lived. The excitement of acquiring new possessions fades quickly as individuals become accustomed to them. This phenomenon, known as hedonic adaptation, explains why the happiness derived from material goods is transient. Hedonic adaptation refers to the process by which individuals return to a relatively stable level of happiness despite major positive or negative events or life changes. When a person buys something new, there is an initial spike in happiness, but over time, the novelty wears off. The initial thrill and pleasure diminish, leading individuals to seek out new acquisitions to recapture that fleeting sense of happiness.

One of the most compelling pieces of evidence for the temporary nature of material satisfaction comes from research on lottery winners. Studies have found that while winning the lottery initially boosts happiness, the effect diminishes over time. Within a year or so, most lottery winners return to their baseline level of happiness, despite their newfound wealth. This suggests that material wealth alone is insufficient to sustain long-term happiness. Material possessions create a cycle of desire that distracts individuals from more enduring sources of happiness. People often find themselves caught in a loop of wanting, acquiring, and then wanting more. This cycle can lead to chronic dissatisfaction, as the temporary joy of new possessions never fully satisfies deeper emotional and psychological needs.

The hedonic treadmill metaphor illustrates the idea that as people achieve more wealth or acquire more possessions, their expectations and desires rise in tandem. This means that the pursuit of happiness through material gains is akin to walking on a treadmill: despite expending effort, individuals do not make any real progress toward sustained happiness. The implications of the hedonic treadmill are significant for understanding the limits of materialism as a path to happiness. It suggests that efforts to achieve happiness through increased consumption are ultimately futile because the satisfaction derived from material goods is fleeting.

Materialism fosters a culture of comparison, where individuals measure their happiness and success against that of others. This comparative mind-set can lead to chronic dissatisfaction and envy, as people often focus on what they lack rather than appreciating what they have. The desire to keep up with or surpass others in terms of material wealth and possessions creates a competitive environment that undermines true happiness. Social comparison theory, developed by psychologist Leon Festinger, explains how individuals determine their own social and personal worth based on how they stack up against others.

In a materialistic culture, this comparison often revolves around possessions, income, and lifestyle. People tend to compare themselves to those who are more affluent or have more luxurious possessions, leading to feelings of inadequacy and envy. The rise of social media has exacerbated this issue, as platforms like Instagram and Facebook create idealized portrayals of others' lives. Users are bombarded with images and posts showcasing the best aspects of others' lives, often showcasing their material successes. This curated reality can distort perceptions, and make it seem as though everyone else is happier and more successful, thus intensifying feelings of inadequacy and dissatisfaction, leading to detrimental effects on mental health. Studies have found correlations between frequent social media use, where individuals are exposed to others' highlight reels, and increased rates of depression, anxiety, and low self-esteem. This is because the constant comparison to others' perceived successes and possessions can make individuals feel as though they are falling short, regardless of their actual circumstances.

The Psychological and Financial Impact of Materialism

One of the primary reasons materialism negatively impacts mental health is that it fosters a never-ending cycle of desire and dissatisfaction. Individuals who prioritize material wealth often find that their happiness is contingent on acquiring the latest products, achieving higher status, or maintaining a certain lifestyle. This constant pursuit creates chronic stress and anxiety, as there is always something more to strive for. The pressure to keep up with societal standards and the perceived success of others exacerbates this stress. Research by psychologists such as Tim Kasser has shown that people with strong materialistic values tend to have poorer mental health outcomes. Kasser's work indicates that materialism is associated with higher levels of anxiety and depression.

One explanation is that materialistic individuals often experience lower quality of interpersonal relationships. The focus on possessions and wealth can lead to neglect of personal connections, often resulting in loneliness and a lack of emotional support. Strong social ties and meaningful relationships are critical components of mental well-being, and their absence can significantly contribute to mental health problems. Furthermore, materialism can lead to unhealthy coping mechanisms. Retail therapy, for instance, becomes a temporary fix for underlying emotional issues, leading to short-lived satisfaction and often financial stress. This coping mechanism can create a vicious cycle, where the temporary relief from purchasing new items quickly fades, leaving individuals feeling emptier and more stressed than before.

The pervasive culture of consumerism also contributes to body image issues and self-esteem problems, particularly in the age of social media. Advertisements and media often promote unrealistic standards of beauty and success and constant comparison to idealized images can result in mental health issues such as body dysmorphia, eating disorders, and chronic dissatisfaction with one's appearance and achievements.

Tying self-worth to material possessions can lead to a fragile sense of identity and self-esteem. In a materialistic society, people often measure their value based on what they own rather than who they are. This external validation is inherently unstable, as it relies on factors outside of one's control and is subject to constant change. When self-worth is contingent on material possessions, individuals may experience significant fluctuations in their self-esteem based on their financial situation. Economic downturns, job loss, or unexpected expenses can severely impact their sense of self, leading to feelings of failure and worthlessness. This fragility stands in stark contrast to a more intrinsic sense of self-worth, which is based on internal values, personal achievements, and self-acceptance.

The emphasis on material possessions can lead to a skewed value system. People may invest excessive time and resources into maintaining an image of success and prosperity, often at the expense of personal growth, relationships, and well-being. A materialistic value system can also lead to unethical behaviour as individuals strive to maintain or enhance their perceived worth.

This might involve compromising personal values, engaging in deceitful practices, or neglecting moral responsibilities. Such actions can create internal conflict and guilt.

One of the most significant consequences of materialism is financially termed as the debt trap. In the pursuit of the latest gadgets, fashion, cars, and homes, individuals often resort to borrowing money. Credit cards, personal loans, and other forms of debt become tools to bridge the gap between desire and financial capability. However, this reliance on credit can quickly spiral out of control. According to the Federal Reserve, the total US consumer debt reached a staggering $4.2 trillion in 2020, a significant portion of which is credit card debt. The ease of obtaining credit, coupled with the pressure to maintain a certain lifestyle, encourages people to spend beyond their means. High-interest rates on credit card debt exacerbate the problem, as individuals find themselves paying substantial amounts in interest alone, often without making a dent in the principal amount owed. The debt trap creates a vicious cycle. People keep accumulating debt, while their financial flexibility decreases, leaving less for savings, investments, and essential expenses. This financial strain can lead to stress and anxiety.

Beyond credit card debt, materialism drives people to take out various types of loans to finance their lifestyle choices. Mortgages, auto loans, and personal loans are common means through which individuals stretch their financial limits to acquire desired assets. While these loans can facilitate important purchases, they also impose long-term financial commitments. Mortgages, for instance, enable homeownership, which is often seen as a foundation stone of the American Dream. However, the pressure to buy larger, more luxurious homes can lead individuals to take on mortgages that exceed their financial capacity.

A significant number of homeowners find themselves 'house poor', spending a large portion of their income on mortgage payments, property taxes, and maintenance. Auto loans are another area in which materialism manifests financially. The desire for new, high-end vehicles drives many to finance cars they cannot afford outright, trapping individuals in loans for vehicles that are worth less than what is owed.

Escaping the Material Trap

Breaking free from materialistic values requires a conscious effort to redefine what constitutes happiness and success. Emphasize personal growth, self-awareness, and internal values over external possessions. Practices such as mindfulness, meditation, and reflective journaling can help individuals reconnect with their inner selves and identify what truly matters to them. Prioritize relationships and social connections over material acquisitions. Spending quality time with family, friends, and the community can provide emotional support and reduce feelings of loneliness.

Develop a habit of gratitude to shift focus from what is lacking to what is already present. Keeping a gratitude journal, where one regularly writes down things they are thankful for, can improve mental health and foster a positive outlook on life. Adopt a minimalist approach to possessions and lifestyle. Simplifying one's environment by decluttering and reducing excess can lead to a greater appreciation of what is truly important. Challenge societal definitions of success that prioritize wealth and status. Develop a personal definition of success that aligns with one's values and aspirations. Practice mindful consumption by being aware of the motives and consequences of purchasing decisions. Before acquiring new items, individuals can ask themselves whether the purchase is necessary and what need it fulfils. Strive for a healthy balance between work and leisure. Overemphasis on work to achieve material success can lead to burnout and neglect of other important aspects of life. Prioritizing leisure activities that bring joy and relaxation, such as hobbies, exercise, and spending time in nature, can improve mental health and provide a more rounded and satisfying life experience.

***

Chapter 17

How to Enjoy Life?

Life is not about waiting for the storm to pass, but learning to dance in the rain

—Vivian Greene

In the bustling narrative of our modern lives, where the cacophony of responsibilities, ambitions, and distractions often drown out the quieter melodies of contentment and joy, the quest to truly enjoy life becomes an elusive pursuit. Life, as Lin Yutang envisioned, is not merely a series of tasks to be accomplished or hurdles to overcome, but a symphony composed of harmonious interplays between our inner selves and the external world. Life's enjoyment lies not merely in the pursuit of fleeting pleasures or momentary happiness, but in the understanding that every experience, whether joyful or challenging, contributes to our existence. It is in the acceptance of impermanence and the embrace of uncertainty that we find liberation.

True enjoyment arises from cultivating a deep connection with ourselves, others, and the world around us – nurturing relationships, exploring our passions, and seeking meaning beyond superficial desires. Through this journey, we come to realize that the essence of life is not found in the accumulation of material wealth or achievements, but in the richness of our experiences and the depth of our connections. It is in this philosophical contemplation that we uncover the beauty of our existence.

Our lives today are characterized by constant movement and incessant noise. From the moment we wake up until the time we finally lay our heads to rest, we are bombarded with information, obligations, and distractions. The digital age has brought unparalleled connectivity but has also blurred the boundaries between work and personal life. This relentless pace can take a toll on our mental and physical well-being, leading to stress, anxiety, and a sense of disconnection from ourselves.

Amidst this chaos, embracing simplicity and serenity becomes a powerful antidote. Simplifying our lives does not necessarily mean stripping away all complexity; rather, it involves prioritizing what truly matters and letting go of the unnecessary. It is about letting go of the constant need for more, the incessant striving for perfection, and instead finding contentment in the present moment. Central to embracing serenity is the cultivation of inner peace. Inner peace is not the absence of challenges or difficulties but rather the ability to remain calm and cantered in the face of them. It is about developing resilience and a sense of perspective that allows us to navigate life's ups and downs with grace and equanimity. Practices such as mindfulness meditation, yoga, or simply taking quiet walks in nature can help cultivate this inner peace, enabling us to tap into a reservoir of calmness even amidst the stormiest of days.

Another way to embrace serenity is by slowing down and appreciating the present moment. In our rush to achieve goals and meet deadlines, we often forget to pause and take in the beauty that surrounds us. Whether it is enjoying a leisurely cup of coffee in the morning, watching the sunset in the evening, or simply breathing deeply and feeling the rhythm of our own heartbeat, these moments of presence are where true serenity resides. When we slow down and embrace serenity, we open ourselves up to savouring life's beauty more fully.

In a world where success is often equated with busyness and productivity, it can be easy to fall into the trap of constant striving and comparison. Serenity offers us a different perspective – a reminder that true fulfilment comes from within, from nurturing our relationships, pursuing our passions, and taking care of our well-being. It encourages us to set boundaries, to say no to things that drain us, and to prioritize self-care as an essential component of a balanced life. Creating physical and emotional spaces that nurture serenity is essential in our journey towards a more balanced and fulfilling life. This could involve designing a peaceful corner in our home where we can retreat and unwind, establishing daily rituals that promote relaxation and self-care, or cultivating relationships that uplift and inspire us.

Coping with Stress and Anxiety

While dealing with our everyday life, we often end up in a vicious whirlwind of stress and anxiety. Enjoying life in this whirlwind then becomes a delicate balancing act between steering through the challenges and nurturing our well-being. While stress can sometimes motivate and drive us forward, chronic stress and overwhelming anxiety can erode us little by little and lead to burnout. Recognizing the signs and symptoms of these conditions is crucial for taking proactive steps towards managing them effectively. Mindfulness meditation is a powerful practice for coping with stress and anxiety. It helps us to learn to observe our thoughts and emotions without judgment, and ground ourselves in the here and now. This helps to quiet the mind, reduce the grip of anxious thoughts, and cultivate a deeper sense of inner peace and clarity. Research consistently demonstrates that regular mindfulness practice can lower stress levels and enhance emotional resilience. Deep breathing exercises offer another effective strategy for managing stress and anxiety by incorporating the intimate connection between our breath and emotional state. Techniques such as diaphragmatic breathing involve slow, deliberate breaths that fill the lungs deeply, followed by complete exhalation. This rhythmic breathing pattern activates the body's relaxation response, reducing physiological symptoms of stress, such as elevated heart rate and muscle tension. Regular practice of deep breathing exercises not only provides immediate relief from acute stress but also enhances respiratory function and promotes a sense of groundedness and centredness in daily life.

Engaging in nurturing hobbies is a meaningful counterbalance to the pressures of everyday life. Whether it is gardening, painting, playing music, or cooking, hobbies provide a sanctuary where we can immerse ourselves in activities that bring us joy. Hobbies promote mindfulness and the flow state – a state of deep concentration and absorption where time seems to suspend. This immersive experience not only enhances our mood but also strengthens our resilience by reinforcing positive emotions and reducing the impact of stressors on our mental health. Coping with stress and anxiety ultimately involves building resilience – our ability to adapt and bounce back from adversity. Resilience is cultivated through a combination of practices and perspectives, including maintaining supportive relationships, adopting a healthy lifestyle with regular exercise and balanced nutrition, and nurturing a positive mind-set through gratitude and self-compassion. Viewing setbacks as opportunities for growth rather than obstacles, we empower ourselves to navigate uncertainty and change more effectively. While self-care practices are valuable, it is important to recognize when professional support may be necessary. If stress or anxiety significantly disrupts daily life, persists despite self-care efforts, or causes significant distress, seeking guidance from a therapist or counsellor can provide strategies and support. Mental health professionals offer evidence-based interventions such as cognitive-behavioural therapy or relaxation techniques to address specific symptoms and underlying causes of stress and anxiety.

Connecting with Nature

Human beings are an integral part of the biodiversity in which they live. No matter how technologically advanced we become, we are inherently connected to the nature that surrounds us. Our existence is intricately intertwined with the natural world – our health, livelihoods, and spiritual well-being depend on the delicate balance of ecosystems. Nature provides us with essential resources, from clean air and water to food and medicine, while also offering solace and inspiration. Spending time in nature holds a unique power to refresh and inspire us. Whether it is a leisurely walk in a local park, a challenging hike in the mountains, or simply sitting by a serene lake, these experiences offer deep connections with the natural world.

Across cultures and throughout history, the connection between humanity and nature has been the basis of spirituality, art, and culture. From ancient civilizations to contemporary societies, the natural world has served as a muse, a source of spiritual reverence, and a canvas for artistic expression. Indigenous cultures around the world exemplify a deep spiritual bond with the land. They view nature as sacred and imbued with spiritual significance. These traditions often emphasize the interconnectedness of all living beings and recognize humans as integral parts of a larger web of life. Practices such as animism, which attributes spiritual qualities to natural elements like trees, rivers, and animals, demonstrate a reverence for the natural world that extends beyond mere material existence. For instance, Native American tribes in North America traditionally hold ceremonies and rituals that honour the spirits of animals and plants, seeking harmony and balance with nature. Similarly, in Aboriginal Australian cultures, the Dreamtime stories convey creation myths and spiritual teachings that emphasize the sacred relationship between humans and the natural environment.

Artists and writers across centuries have drawn inspiration from nature's beauty, using their craft to capture its essence and evoke profound emotional responses. In visual arts, landscapes have long been a prominent subject to reflect not only physical features but also the artist's emotional and spiritual connection to the natural world. From the Romantic painters of the nineteenth century, who idealized nature as a sublime force, to contemporary environmental artists advocating for conservation through their works, nature continues to inspire creativity and evoke awe. Poetry, too, has celebrated nature's beauty and served as a medium for exploring humanity's relationship with the natural world. Poets like William Wordsworth, John Keats, and Emily Dickinson found solace and inspiration in the landscapes around them. They wove elaborate themes of transcendence, mortality, and the sublime into their verses. Their poems resonate with a reverence for nature's grandeur and a recognition of its capacity to evoke spiritual and emotional transformation. Similarly, in literature, natural settings often serve as symbolic backdrops that mirror characters' inner journeys or societal changes. From Shakespeare's forests in *A Midsummer Night's Dream* to the rugged wilderness of Jack London's *The Call of the Wild*, authors use nature to convey themes of freedom, renewal, and the resilience of the human spirit. Contemporary fiction continues this tradition, while exploring ecological themes and the impact of human activities on natural ecosystems.

Beyond individual artistic endeavours, cultural traditions and rituals worldwide reflect a deep respect for nature's rhythms and cycles. Festivals celebrating seasonal changes, agricultural rites of passage, and ceremonies honouring ancestral lands are integral parts of many cultures. For example, the Japanese tradition of Hanami, or cherry blossom viewing, celebrates the ephemeral beauty of cherry blossoms each spring. Families and friends gather under blooming trees to appreciate their fleeting splendour, reflecting a deep appreciation for the transience of natural cycles. In Hinduism, festivals like Diwali and Holi are rooted in mythological narratives that symbolize the triumph of good over evil and the renewal of life, often incorporating rituals performed outdoors amidst natural elements.

Nature has long been known for its ability to heal and rejuvenate. Being in natural surroundings can reduce stress levels, lower blood pressure, and improve our wellbeing. The sight of sunlight filtering through leaves, the sound of birdsong, or the scent of pine trees, nature engages our senses in ways that calm and centre us. It encourages us to slow down, breathe deeply, and appreciate the present moment. Walking through a forest or gazing at a starlit sky can evoke a sense of wonder and humility, reminding us of the vastness and beauty of the universe beyond our daily concerns. Nature provides a space for introspection and reflection, where we can gain perspective on our lives and reconnect with what truly matters. Engaging with nature does not always require elaborate plans or travel. It can be as simple as watching clouds drift across the sky, feeling the warmth of the sun on your face, or listening to the rhythmic crash of ocean waves. These moments of quiet observation and appreciation can bring a sense of peace and contentment that is both grounding and uplifting. When we witness the beauty and diversity of natural landscapes, from mountains and forests to rivers and oceans, we develop a greater understanding of the delicate balance of ecosystems. This awareness can inspire us to make choices that minimize our impact on the environment and support conservation efforts for future generations.

Pursuing Passion and Creativity

Igniting our passion and creativity is fundamental to leading a fulfilling life, one that goes beyond mere existence to embrace meaningful experiences and personal growth. Whether through hobbies, artistic pursuits, or intellectual endeavours, these activities offer pathways to self-discovery and fulfilment. For some, this might involve immersing oneself in the world of visual arts – painting landscapes that evoke emotions or sculpting forms that capture the essence of humanity. For others, it could mean delving into the intricate melodies of music, the rhythmic dance movements that express narratives, or the meticulous crafting of stories that resonate with universal truths. Often, these inclinations are overshadowed by the busyness of life. Reigniting these passions can bring back the childish joy and peace.

Creativity is not confined to traditional artistic mediums; it permeates every aspect of human endeavour. It manifests in problem-solving, innovation, and the ability to envision possibilities beyond the status quo. Creative expression allows individuals to communicate their innermost thoughts, emotions, and perspectives in ways that transcend language and cultural boundaries. It enables them to challenge conventions, explore alternative viewpoints, and contribute novel insights to society. For instance, engineers and scientists harness creativity to design ground-breaking technologies that improve lives and address global challenges. Entrepreneurs infuse creativity into their business ventures, shaping innovative products and services that meet evolving consumer needs. In educational settings, teachers employ creative teaching methods to engage students and foster a passion for learning. Creativity, therefore, serves as a catalyst for personal and societal transformation, driving progress and enriching human experiences across diverse domains.

Engaging in passion-driven activities offers a myriad of benefits that extend beyond personal fulfilment. Pursuing hobbies and creative pursuits can promote mental well-being by reducing stress, anxiety, and depression. These activities provide opportunities for relaxation, mindfulness, and emotional catharsis, which can enable individuals to recharge and maintain a healthy work-life balance. They stimulate cognitive function, enhance problem-solving skills, and foster lifelong learning – an essential component of personal development and adaptability in an increasingly complex world. Furthermore, such endeavours often create opportunities for social connection and community engagement. Shared interests bring individuals together, fostering friendships, collaboration, and a sense of belonging.

Living a creative lifestyle involves weaving passion and artistic expression into the fabric of everyday existence through deliberate choices and habits that foster personal growth and holistic well-being. It is about carving out dedicated moments amidst the hustle of daily life to engage in activities that ignite inspiration and nourish the soul. Curiosity and a spirit of experimentation are essential companions on this journey. They beckon us to explore uncharted territories, embrace new techniques, and view the world through fresh lenses. By seeking inspiration from a myriad of sources – be it the intricate brushstrokes of a painting, the lyrical prose of a novel, the serene beauty of nature's landscapes, or the fleeting moments of everyday life – we replenish our creative reservoirs and spark innovative ideas. Connecting with a community of kindred spirits amplifies our creative experience. Whether joining clubs, participating in workshops, or engaging in online forums, these platforms offer fertile ground for collaboration, feedback, and the exchange of insights. Yet, amidst the pursuit of creativity, self-care remains paramount. It involves honouring the body and mind with rest, relaxation, and activities that promote well-being. This deliberate balance sustains our creative energies and guards against the perils of burnout, and ensures that our artistic pursuits remain vibrant and enduring. It invites us to explore the depths of our potential, discover new facets of self-expression, and revel in the joy of artistic discovery.

***

Chapter 17

Experiencing Life through Travel and Culture

Travel far enough, you meet yourself

—David Mitchell

In the quiet corners of our minds, there exists a longing – an inexplicable yearning that tugs at our hearts when we gaze at maps or hear tales of far-off lands. It is a feeling that transcends mere curiosity; it is the magnetic pull of wanderlust, the deep-seated desire to break free from the routine and familiar, to venture into the unknown and immerse ourselves in the vast tapestry of the world. Wanderlust is a quest for discovery, a yearning to experience different cultures, landscapes, and perspectives. It draws us out of our comfort zones and challenges us to embrace the unfamiliar.

Each journey becomes a canvas on which we paint our stories and blend with the hues of distant sunsets, the aromas of exotic spices, and the melodies of foreign tongues. The call of the unknown is a powerful force. It arising from a restlessness that cannot be appeased by the routines of daily life. It is a call to adventure, beckoning us to step beyond the boundaries of our familiar existence and into the vastness of the world.

For some, wanderlust manifests as a yearning for escape. It is a temporary reprieve from the responsibilities and expectations that anchor us to our daily lives. It offers a sanctuary where time slows down, and the mind finds solace in the simplicity of living moment to moment. Yet, wanderlust is not merely about physical travel; it is a state of mind, a perpetual curiosity that drives us to seek out new experiences and expand our understanding of the world. Lin Yutang's observation that the true beauty of travel is often realized upon returning home speaks to a deeper truth: that the journey outward is also a journey inward, a reflection of our evolving selves. Travel becomes a mirror that reflects our strengths and vulnerabilities, our prejudices and preconceptions. It invites introspection as we navigate foreign streets and navigate unfamiliar customs. It prompts us to confront our own biases and embrace the diversity of human existence.

Travel is often portrayed as a series of destinations to be checked off a list, captured in photographs, and recounted in anecdotes. However, beneath the surface of this superficial tourism lies a deeper, more enriching experience: cultural immersion. Beyond sightseeing, cultural immersion is about forging connections, embracing differences, and delving into the soul of a society. One of the richest threads is woven through the act of sampling local cuisine. Food is more than sustenance; it is a gateway to understanding history, geography, and social customs. Each dish tells a story, a tale of local ingredients, culinary techniques passed down through generations, and the fusion of flavours that define a region's identity. Stepping into a bustling market or a humble street stall, travellers are greeted not just by the aromas of spices and simmering pots but by the warmth of hospitality that transcends language barriers. Sharing a meal with locals becomes a ritual of communion, a chance to savour not only the food but also stories and traditions.

Similarly, learning traditional dances or participating in cultural performances offer a visceral connection to the heartbeat of a community. Dance is a universal language of expression, embodying history, emotions, and collective memories. Whether it's the rhythmic stomping of flamenco in Spain, the graceful movements of a Balinese Legong dance, or the spirited twirls of a folk dance in the Balkans; each step tells a tale of resilience, celebration, and cultural pride.

Cultural immersion extends beyond scheduled activities into spontaneous moments of connection and understanding. It is the late-night conversations with locals under starlit skies, where stories flow freely like the constellations above. Sitting around a campfire in the Sahara Desert, listening to Berber tales passed down through generations, or sharing laughter over steaming cups of tea in a Japanese tea house. These are the moments that etch themselves into the traveller's memory, forging bonds that transcend language and cultural differences. In these exchanges, stereotypes dissolve, and empathy blooms, a recognition of our shared humanity amidst the tapestry of diversity that colours our world.

This immersion is not without its challenges and discomforts. It demands humility, to acknowledge one's status as a guest in another's homeland and adaptability to navigate unfamiliar social norms and etiquettes. Yet, it is precisely these challenges that pave the way for personal growth. Authenticity is paramount in immersing in local cultures. It is a commitment to engage with communities on their own terms and respecting traditions while fostering genuine connections.

Reflections on Home and Identity

As travellers, we embark on journeys that span continents and traverse oceans and carry with us not just our belongings but also our identities – fragments of our past, aspirations for the future, and the memories that define our sense of home.

Home, for many, is more than a physical place; it is a sanctuary of memories, traditions, and the people who shape our lives. It is the familiar scent of childhood meals wafting from the kitchen, the comfort of well-worn pathways through familiar neighbourhoods, and the reassuring embrace of loved ones. Yet, as we venture beyond these familiar boundaries, we begin to unravel the intricacies of our identities, woven from the threads of cultural heritage and personal experiences. Travel reshapes our understanding of home by juxtaposing the familiar with the unfamiliar. It invites us to appreciate the richness of diversity while deepening our appreciation for the comforts of familiarity. It is in the bustling markets of Marrakech, where the aroma of spices mingles with the vibrant colours of textiles, that we discover echoes of our own cultural vibrancy. It is in the tranquil temples of Kyoto, where in the ritual of tea ceremony, we find resonance with our own rituals of familial bonding. In the labyrinthine streets of Istanbul, where East meets West in a symphony of cultural fusion, we witness the fluidity of identity. Amidst the exhilaration of exploration, travel also evokes a poignant sense of longing. In these moments of nostalgia, we come to appreciate the intangible elements that define our sense of belonging. It is through this juxtaposition of longing and discovery that we cultivate a deeper understanding of our own identities.

Being Spontaneous

Serendipity is a guiding force of travellers. It is a subtle hand that orchestrates encounters and unveils hidden treasures along the journey of travel. Travel, often associated with meticulous planning and structured agendas, paradoxically offers some of its most beautiful experiences in unplanned moments. Serendipity manifests in myriad forms: a chance encounter with a wise old storyteller in a bustling market, stumbling upon a hidden gem of a café down a winding alley, or finding oneself swept into a local festival by the rhythms of distant drums. The essence of serendipity lies in its unpredictability, a reminder that life's most precious gifts often arrive when least expected. It challenges us to surrender control and embrace uncertainty. It invites us to trust in the rhythm of the universe and the interconnectedness of our paths with those we meet along the way. Serendipity promotes a sense of presence, an acute awareness of the present moment, and an openness to the possibilities that unfold before us. It encourages us to listen attentively to the stories shared by strangers, and to embrace the spontaneity that breathes life into our experiences.

Being spontaneous is an art. It wants us to release our attachment to rigid schedules and predetermined outcomes. It encourages us to follow our intuition and trust in the innate wisdom that guides us towards unforeseen encounters and serendipitous discoveries. Imagine standing at a bustling train station in a foreign city, gazing at a departure board adorned with exotic names. In that moment, spontaneity beckons. A sudden impulse takes hold – a train to a quaint village in the countryside rather than the bustling metropolis you had planned. This decision is not guided by guidebooks or internet reviews, but by a desire for the thrill of the unknown. Yet spontaneity in travel is not merely about making impulsive decisions; it is a mind-set that encourages openness and flexibility. One of the most beautiful aspects of spontaneous travel is its ability to cultivate genuine connections. When plans are fluid, interactions with locals become more meaningful. Conversations unfold naturally, unburdened by the rush of a tightly scheduled itinerary. Shared meals, spontaneous celebrations, and moments of laughter become the souvenirs that linger long after the trip has ended. Spontaneity also invites a deeper immersion into the local culture. It encourages travellers to engage with their surroundings on a visceral level, to explore beyond the tourist hotspots, and to discover the heartbeat of a place. It also fosters a sense of liberation and empowerment. In these moments, the fear of the unknown transforms into exhilaration, as each twist and turn unfold with the promise of new horizons. Of course, embracing spontaneity in travel requires a balance of mindfulness and intuition. It's about being attuned to one's surroundings, recognizing opportunities as they arise, and assessing risks with a discerning eye. It is not reckless abandon but rather a balance between curiosity and caution. However, spontaneity does not necessarily imply a complete departure from planning. Rather, it complements structured travel arrangements, while adding depth and richness to the overall experience.

An Expedition Within Oneself

Travelling is also a journey of self-discovery. It is a pilgrimage to the inner recesses of our own being. It strips away the layers of societal roles and expectations and reveals our true essence beneath. Removed from the familiar constraints of home, we are liberated to explore facets of ourselves previously unknown or suppressed. In the solitude of a foreign landscape, introspection becomes a companion. Moments of clarity emerge like stars in a darkened sky. We confront fears and insecurities, confront weaknesses, and celebrate strengths. This process of self-discovery nurtures personal growth and empowers us to embrace change with courage and conviction. The fear of failure, once a dormant ember, blazes into a fire of determination. In its glow, we uncover reservoirs of resilience and creativity previously untapped. Personal growth thrives amidst the challenges of self-discovery. It is nurtured by the sunlight of introspection and the nourishment of new experiences. As we cultivate awareness, we cultivate compassion – for ourselves and for others.

Travelling across different cultures is akin to opening a treasure trove of diversity, where each encounter unfolds a new facet of humanity. It is through these interactions that our perspectives expand, our thoughts deepen, and our capacity for tolerance blossoms. When we immerse ourselves in unfamiliar customs and traditions, we are confronted with perspectives that challenge our preconceived notions. Language, too, serves as a gateway to understanding. Learning a new one allows us to connect with others on a deeper level. Perhaps most importantly, cultural immersion nurtures tolerance by fostering empathy and respect for difference. As we encounter complexities of cross-cultural communication, we learn to navigate ambiguity and uncertainty with grace. We embrace the discomfort of cultural dissonance as an opportunity for growth and recognize that true understanding is born not from uniformity but from diversity. In a world increasingly interconnected yet divided, the lessons learned through cultural exploration are more pertinent than ever. They remind us that beneath the surface of diversity lies a shared humanity.

Further, travelling compels us to confront our biases and confront the assumptions we hold about others. Each encounter becomes a mirror reflecting our own cultural conditioning and biases, prompting us to question deeply ingrained beliefs. Thus, travel fosters a sense of humility as we witness the vastness of the world and our small place within it. Standing amidst towering mountains or expansive deserts, we are reminded of the insignificance of our individual concerns in the grand scheme of the universe. This humbling realization instills a sense of awe and wonder, sparking a curiosity that transcends borders and encourages lifelong learning. Once we understand this, travelling then serves as a catalyst for creativity and innovation. In the midst of unfamiliar surroundings, we are inspired by the novel sights, sounds, and flavours that stimulate our senses and ignite our imagination. This creative expression not only enhances our journey, but also becomes a tangible record of our personal growth and evolution.

***

Chapter 18

Connection to God

We need to find God, and he cannot be found in noise and restlessness. God is the friend of silence.

—Mother Teresa

The search for divinity is a journey as old as humanity itself. From the dawn of civilization, humans have sought to understand and connect with a higher power, to make sense of the vast mysteries of existence and find a place within the cosmic order. The divine is not a distant, unreachable entity, but rather an integral part of the world around us. By appreciating the small, often overlooked details of our daily existence, we can tap into a source of spiritual insight. The divine is accessible in the ordinary, in the routine moments that make up our lives.

Divinity lies the intrinsic desire to connect with something greater than ourselves. This yearning is a fundamental aspect of the human condition. True fulfilment comes from a life lived in harmony with nature and with others. This harmonious existence is not about renouncing the world but embracing it fully, with all its beauty and imperfections. The connection to the divine is deeply rooted in the principles of living in accordance with the fundamental nature of the universe. It is about aligning ourselves with this natural order so that we can achieve a state of harmony. This alignment is not achieved through rigid adherence to dogma or ritual, but through a flexible, intuitive understanding of life's natural rhythms. The divine is accessible to everyone, regardless of their religious or spiritual background.

The quest for divinity is a personal journey and unique to each individual. It encourages us to find our own path to the divine, one that resonates with our personal experiences and beliefs. It is a journey that requires introspection and open-mindedness. In this fast-paced world, the search for divinity can often feel like an elusive goal. We are bombarded with distractions and pressures that pull us away from our inner selves and our connection to the divine. To counterbalance this frenetic pace of life, it is essential to slow down, appreciate the present moment, and find joy in the simple pleasures of existence. It is about finding the courage to live a life that is true to our values and beliefs, even if it means going against the grain. The search for divinity is not a linear journey with a clear destination, but a continuous process of growth and self-discovery. It is about finding beauty and meaning in the everyday, about connecting with the world around us and with our inner selves. It is about living a life that is rich in experiences, relationships, and moments of quiet contemplation.

Nature as a Reflection of the Divine

In the quiet majesty of a forest, the rhythmic ebb and flow of the ocean, or the delicate bloom of a flower, one can sense the presence of something greater than oneself. Nature, in all its splendor and subtlety, offers a profound source of spiritual insight. It serves as a mirror reflecting the divine. The cycle of the seasons, with their birth, growth, decay, and rebirth, echoes the spiritual cycles of human life. Spring's rejuvenation reminds us of renewal and hope, while autumn's decay speaks to the inevitability of change and the beauty in endings. Each season holds lessons about the divine nature of existence, illustrating the impermanence and continuity that characterize both the natural world and our spiritual journeys. Consider the mountains, standing tall and silent. They represent steadfastness, strength, and endurance. Their peaks, often shrouded in clouds, suggest the transcendence of the human spirit, reaching towards the heavens. Mountains remind us of the divine heights we aspire to, the challenges we must overcome, and the serenity found in stillness. In contrast, valleys, with their lush, fertile grounds, symbolize abundance, nurturing, and the embrace of life's lows as opportunities for growth and reflection.

Water, with its fluidity and adaptability, serves as another metaphor for the divine. Rivers carve through landscapes, symbolizing life's journey, persistence, and the passage of time. The ocean, vast and unfathomable, reflects the infinite and mysterious nature of the divine. Its waves, ever-changing yet eternal, remind us of the constant motion and transformation inherent in both nature and spiritual life. Standing on the shore, gazing at the horizon where sea meets sky, we are reminded of the interconnectedness of all things, the seamless blend of the physical and the spiritual. In the stillness of a forest, we encounter the divine in the intricate web of life that thrives in its depths. Each tree, plant, and animal plays a role in a complex ecosystem, reflecting the interconnectedness and interdependence of all existence. The forest's canopy shelters life below, while its roots reach deep into the earth, drawing sustenance from unseen sources. This hidden network mirrors the unseen threads that connect us to the divine. The sky, with its ever-changing canvas, offers a daily testament to the divine's presence. The breath-taking displays of colour and light at sunrises and sunsets symbolize the continuous cycle of beginnings and endings. The sun rises each day, bringing light and warmth, dispelling darkness, and nurturing growth. The night sky, with its vast expanse of stars, evokes wonder and awe, reminding us of our smallness in the grand scheme of the universe and the boundless possibilities that lie beyond our comprehension.

This natural world operates on principles of harmony and balance. In nature, everything exists in a state of dynamic equilibrium. The balance between predator and prey, the ebb and flow of tides, the cycle of growth and decay – all illustrate the delicate balance that sustains life. This natural harmony reflects the divine order, suggesting that balance and moderation are key to spiritual well-being. The Taoist perspective teaches that by living in harmony with nature, we align ourselves with the divine. This harmony is not about imposing our will on the natural world, but about attuning ourselves to its rhythms and flows. It involves recognizing the interconnectedness of all things and understanding that our actions have consequences that ripple through the web of life. This awareness nurtures a sense of humility and reverence for the natural world. Just as nature seeks equilibrium, so too must we strive for balance within ourselves. This means acknowledging and integrating all aspects of our being – our strengths and weaknesses, our joys and sorrows, our desires and fears. It involves cultivating a state of inner peace and stillness, akin to the calm surface of a lake that reflects the sky above. In this state of balance, we are better able to hear the quiet whisper of the divine.

The Divine Connection with the Inner Self

Connecting with the divine is often portrayed as a journey that requires looking inward rather than outward. This inward journey is a path of introspection and self-awareness. It is a journey that invites us to explore the depths of our own consciousness, to confront our fears and desires, and to find a sense of inner peace that aligns us with a higher power. The idea of an inward journey suggests that the divine is not a distant, external entity, but an intimate presence within us. This perspective challenges us to look beyond the surface of our everyday experiences and to seek the sacred in the quiet, hidden corners of our own hearts and minds. It is in these quiet spaces that we can encounter the divine, not as an abstract concept but as a living reality that informs and enriches our lives. Introspection and self-awareness are key components of this inward journey. By turning our gaze inward, we can begin to understand the intricate workings of our own minds and hearts. This process requires honesty and courage, as it often involves confronting aspects of ourselves. Yet, it is through this confrontation that we can achieve greater clarity and insight, allowing us to transcend our limitations and connect more deeply with the divine. Self-awareness is not just about recognizing our flaws and weaknesses; it is also about acknowledging our strengths and potential as well.

It involves developing a balanced and compassionate understanding of who we are, accepting ourselves fully, and striving to grow and improve. This holistic self-awareness creates a foundation for spiritual growth. This inward journey is also about cultivating a sense of presence and mindfulness. By being fully present in each moment, we can become more attuned to the subtle movements of our own thoughts and feelings, as well as the signs and signals of the divine.

Meditation and contemplation are powerful practices that can facilitate this inward journey. These practices help us to quiet the mind and develop a deeper awareness of our inner landscape. Meditation involves focusing the mind on a single point of reference, such as the breath, a mantra, or an image. This practice helps to calm the incessant chatter of the mind, creating a space of stillness and clarity. Through regular meditation, we can develop a greater sense of inner peace and stability, which can enhance our ability to connect with the divine. There are different forms of meditation, each with its own unique benefits. Mindfulness meditation, for example, involves paying attention to the present moment without judgment, allowing us to experience life more fully and directly. This practice can help us to develop a deeper awareness of our thoughts, feelings, and sensations. Loving-kindness meditation, on the other hand, involves cultivating feelings of compassion and love towards ourselves and others. This practice can help to open our hearts, fostering a sense of connection and empathy that can enhance our relationship with the divine. Contemplation, like meditation, involves focusing the mind, but it is often more reflective in nature. Contemplative practices might include reading and reflecting on spiritual texts, engaging in deep thought about philosophical or theological questions, or simply sitting in silence and pondering the mysteries of existence.

Yogis, the practitioners of ancient spiritual traditions, have long pursued the path to divinity through meditation. This practice, deeply rooted in the philosophy of yoga, seeks to unite the individual soul with the universal consciousness, often referred to as Brahman or the divine. Meditation, or *Dhyana*, is one of the eight limbs of yoga as outlined by the sage Patanjali in the Yoga Sutras. It is a practice that involves focused concentration and deep contemplation. For yogis, meditation is not merely a technique but a way of life, a disciplined practice that leads to the purification of the mind and the unfolding of spiritual consciousness. The initial stages of meditation involve calming the mind and withdrawing the senses from the external world, a process known as *Pratyahara.* By turning inward, yogis learn to quiet the constant chatter of thoughts and emotions. This state of inner silence is essential for achieving deeper levels of concentration, or *Dharana.* Through sustained focus on a single point of reference, such as the breath, a mantra, or an image, the mind becomes still and serene. This inner peace is the foundation upon which yogis build their spiritual practice. It allows them to transcend the distractions and disturbances of the external world, creating a space where they can connect with their true selves. In this tranquil state, the mind becomes a clear mirror, reflecting the deeper truths of existence.

As meditation deepens, yogis move beyond the calm of Dharana into the state of Dhyana. Here, the distinction between the meditator and the object of meditation begins to dissolve. The yogi enters a state of flow, where the mind is fully absorbed in the meditative focus, leading to a profound sense of unity and clarity. This stage is crucial for self-realization, the recognition of one's true nature. In the philosophy of yoga, this true nature is often referred to as the *Atman*, or the inner self. Through deep meditation, yogis experience the Atman directly, realizing that it is identical with Brahman, the universal consciousness. This realization is a transformative experience, breaking down the illusion of separateness and revealing the interconnectedness of all life.

The ultimate goal of yogic meditation is to achieve *samadhi*, the state of union with the divine. In samadhi, the yogi transcends the limitations of the physical and mental realms, merging completely with the universal consciousness. This state is characterized by an overwhelming sense of peace, joy, and unity. The individual ego dissolves, and the yogi experiences oneness with all of existence. In this state of divine union, the boundaries between self and other, between individual and cosmos, disappear. The yogi realizes that the divine is not an external entity to be reached or worshipped from afar but is inherent in every aspect of existence, including within themselves. This realization is the essence of enlightenment in the yogic tradition.

The benefits of meditation extend beyond the moments spent in deep contemplation. For yogis, the insights and tranquility gained through meditation permeate all aspects of life. They carry a sense of inner peace and clarity into their daily activities, interactions, and decisions. This balanced state of mind enables them to live in harmony with themselves and the world around them, embodying the principles of compassion, wisdom, and selflessness. Meditation and contemplation help us to develop a serene and balanced mind in a world that is often chaotic and stressful. The practice of meditation and contemplation help to deepen our relationship with the divine by fostering a sense of humility and surrender. These practices can help us to cultivate a sense of gratitude and appreciation for the present moment. In addition to their spiritual benefits, meditation and contemplation can also have beneficiary effects on our physical and mental health. As we continue on this inward journey, let us remember that the path to spiritual fulfilment is not a destination but a continuous process of growth and discovery. Each moment offers an opportunity to deepen our connection to the divine, to cultivate inner peace, and to live more fully and authentically.

Cultural Perspectives on Divinity

The concept of divinity and the ways in which humans seek to connect with it vary widely across cultures, particularly between Eastern and Western philosophies. This diversity offers a richness of beliefs, practices, and insights that reflect the unique perspectives from which they arise. Yet, despite these differences, there is a shared, underlying quest for understanding and connection with the divine that unites humanity. Eastern philosophies often emphasize the immanence of the divine, suggesting that divinity permeates all aspects of existence. In Hinduism, for example, God is both transcendent and immanent, present in every atom of creation and yet beyond all. The concept of Brahman represents the ultimate, unchanging reality amidst and beyond the world, while Atman, the inner self or soul, is seen as a reflection of Brahman within each individual. Similarly, in Buddhism, while the focus is less on a personal God and more on achieving enlightenment, there is a deep recognition of interconnectedness and the divine nature of the universe. In Taoism, the *Tao* (or *Dao*) is the fundamental principle that is the source of everything and that lies behind the natural order of the universe. The Tao is not a deity in the traditional sense but a path or way that individuals should seek to align themselves with to achieve harmony and balance.

In contrast, Western philosophies of God often emphasize a more personal and transcendent conception of the divine. In Christianity, God is seen as a personal, omniscient, omnipotent being who created the universe and continues to interact with it. The relationship between the individual and God is often portrayed as a personal relationship, characterized by prayer, worship, and a moral code derived from divine commandments. Judaism and Islam also emphasize the transcendence of God but include elements of immanence and personal connection. In Judaism, God is both the creator of the universe and a personal deity who enters into covenants with His people. In Islam, Allah is the all-powerful and all-knowing creator, yet believers are encouraged to develop a personal relationship with Him through practices such as prayer (*salah*) and remembrance (*dhikr*).

These varying perspectives highlight the diverse ways cultures approach the concept of divinity. Eastern philosophies often focus on understanding and harmonizing with the divine order of the universe, while Western philosophies emphasize a personal, relational aspect with a transcendent God. Despite these differences, both traditions seek to understand the divine and our place within the cosmos. There are common threads that unite various religious and spiritual traditions. One common thread is the concept of the sacred or the holy, which is central to all spiritual traditions. Whether it is the sanctity of nature in indigenous religions, the holiness of God in monotheistic faiths, or the sacredness of life in Eastern philosophies, there is a universal recognition of something greater than the individual that inspires awe, reverence, and a sense of the sublime. Another universal aspect is the transformative power of spiritual practice. Practices such as meditation, prayer, contemplation, and ritual are found in nearly all spiritual traditions. Most spiritual traditions also emphasize the importance of love, compassion, and ethical behaviour as pathways to connect with the divine.

In Christianity, the teachings of Jesus emphasize love and compassion for others. In Buddhism, the practice of compassion (*karuna*) and loving-kindness (*metta*) is central to achieving enlightenment. In Hinduism, the concept of *Ahimsa*, or non-violence, is a fundamental ethical principle. The search for meaning and purpose is a universal spiritual quest. Whether it is through understanding one's Dharma in Hinduism, seeking *Nirvana* in Buddhism, following God's will in Islam, or living a righteous life in Christianity, individuals across cultures seek to understand their purpose and align their lives with a greater cosmic or divine order.

Art and literature have long been recognized as mediums for experiencing and expressing the divine. Through creativity, artists and writers capture the ineffable, translating spiritual experiences and insights into tangible forms, allowing us to glimpse the divine through beauty and symbolism. The intricate mandalas of Tibetan Buddhism, for example, are visual representations of the universe and serve as tools for meditation and spiritual teaching. The frescoes of the Sistine Chapel depict biblical scenes with profound theological significance, drawing viewers into a contemplation of divine mysteries. In these ways, art transcends the ordinary, offering a window into the sacred and inviting viewers into a deeper spiritual engagement. Literature, too, serves as a vehicle for exploring and expressing the divine. Poets like Rumi and mystics like Teresa of Avila used their words to convey their intimate experiences of God. Their writings evoke a sense of the divine, inviting readers to reflect on their own spiritual experiences and aspirations. Art and literature also bridge cultural and religious divides as themes of love, suffering, redemption, and transcendence found in sacred texts, poetry, and stories resonate across different traditions.

Sacredness in Daily Life

Living with a sense of the sacred involves recognizing and honouring the divine in the ordinary moments of daily life. It is about cultivating an awareness that every action, no matter how mundane, can be imbued with spiritual significance. When we treat our daily activities with reverence, we transform the ordinary into the extraordinary. A morning cup of tea, a walk in the park, or a conversation with a loved one becomes an opportunity to connect with the sacred. This perspective aligns with the idea that life itself is a gift, and each moment is precious. Embracing the sacredness of daily life means recognizing the beauty and wonder that surround us, even in the most routine activities. It invites us to see the divine not as a distant entity, but as an ever-present reality that permeates all aspects of our existence. To cultivate a sense of the sacred in everyday life, it can be helpful to incorporate simple rituals and practices that hold personal meaning. These rituals do not need to be elaborate or prescriptive; rather, they should be flexible and adaptable to individual preferences and lifestyles. The goal is to create moments of intentionality and mindfulness that remind us of the sacredness of life. One effective practice is the creation of a morning or evening ritual. This could include lighting a candle, saying a prayer or affirmation, or spending a few minutes in quiet meditation. Such rituals set a tone of reverence and mindfulness for the day ahead or provide a peaceful transition into rest. Another practice is mindful eating. By paying full attention to the process of preparing and consuming food, we can transform a daily necessity into a sacred act. This involves appreciating the colours, textures, and flavours of the food, as well as expressing gratitude for the nourishment it provides. Mindful eating encourages us to slow down and savour each bite, encouraging a deeper connection with the present moment and the life-sustaining energy of food. Spending time in nature is another powerful way to experience the sacred. Nature's beauty and tranquillity can inspire awe and reverence, reminding us of the interconnectedness of all life and our place within the greater whole. Creative expression through activities such as painting, writing, or playing music allows us to tap into our creative spirit and channel it into forms that reflect our inner experiences. Practicing gratitude is a simple yet profound way to cultivate a sense of the sacred. Taking time each day to reflect on the things we are grateful for helps to shift our focus from what is lacking to what is abundant.

***

Chapter 19

The Art of Thinking

The world as we have created it is a process of our thinking. It cannot be changed without changing our thinking.

—Albert Einstein

Thinking is more than a mere cognitive process; it is an art form that shapes our understanding of the world and ourselves. Thinking involves mental processes, such as reasoning, problem-solving, decision-making, and imagination. These processes are fundamental to human cognition and are often considered the distinguishing characteristics of our species. However, thinking is not merely a biological function but a complex interaction of conscious and unconscious activities that shape our perception and interpretation of the world. Philosophers throughout history have grappled with the nature of thinking. From Aristotle's emphasis on logic and categorization to Descartes' exploration of doubt and certainty, various thinkers have provided frameworks to understand how we think and what constitutes valid reasoning. The art of thinking, therefore, encompasses not only the ability to process information but also to critically evaluate ideas, explore possibilities, and synthesize new insights.

Human thought process is multidimensional. Epistemological dimension of thinking explores how we acquire knowledge and justify beliefs. Epistemology investigates questions of truth, the reliability of our senses, and the methods used to distinguish reality from illusion. Here, the emphasis is on discerning between well-founded beliefs and mere opinions, which fosters intellectual virtues like open-mindedness and intellectual humility. Ethical dimension suggests that ethics influence the subjects we ponder and how we engage intellectually. It involves reflecting on our moral responsibilities, considering how our thoughts impact others, and scrutinizing the ethical implications embedded in our beliefs. Ethical thinking requires us to assess the consequences of our ideas and strive for moral clarity in our reasoning.

Existential dimension touches on our self-understanding and our place in the world. Existentialist thinkers, such as Sartre and Kierkegaard, examined how thinking shapes our identity, freedom, and search for meaning. Thinking existentially involves dealing with questions of authenticity, confronting feelings of alienation, and seeking purpose in the face of life's uncertainties. It necessitates introspection into fundamental aspects of human existence. Together, these dimensions illustrate the richness and complexity of thinking as a fundamental human activity.

What, then, makes thinking an art? Artistry in thinking goes beyond mere technical proficiency; it involves creativity, intuition, and the ability to see connections where others might not. Just as a painter uses brushes and colours to create a masterpiece, a thinker employs concepts and ideas to craft new insights and understandings. Creativity is central to the art of thinking. It involves the ability to generate novel ideas, make unexpected connections. Creative thinking challenges established norms and encourages exploration of alternative perspectives. It is through creativity that new paradigms are born, scientific discoveries are made, and artistic expressions are realized. Insight, on the other hand, is the sudden realization or deep understanding that transcends ordinary thought. Insights often arise unexpectedly, triggered by a combination of subconscious processing and focused contemplation. The art of thinking includes cultivating conditions that facilitate moments of insight, such as periods of reflection, exposure to diverse perspectives, and a willingness to question assumptions. Intuition involves the ability to grasp truths or make decisions without conscious reasoning. While intuition can be informed by experience and knowledge, it also relies on unconscious processes that are difficult to articulate. The art of thinking intuitively requires developing sensitivity to subtle cues, trusting one's instincts, and discerning when to rely on intuition versus deliberate reasoning. Judgment is the capacity to assess the validity and relevance of ideas. It requires intellectual honesty, scepticism towards unsubstantiated claims, and a willingness to revise one's beliefs in light of new information. Good judgment emerges from a combination of cognitive rigour and ethical discernment.

The Power of Thinking Beyond the Ordinary

In our journey through life, there comes a point where the ordinary no longer suffices. It is at this juncture that we find ourselves drawn to explore beyond the obvious. Thinking beyond the obvious is akin to exploring uncharted waters where imagination reigns supreme. Consider the pioneering work of Nikola Tesla, whose visionary ideas about electricity and wireless communication laid the foundation for much of our modern technology. Tesla's ability to envision a world powered by alternating current and his relentless pursuit of unconventional solutions transformed the whole landscape of engineering and communication for eternity. Similarly, the architectural marvels of Antoni Gaudí in Barcelona stand as testament to thinking beyond traditional boundaries. Gaudí's unique approach to design, blending natural forms with innovative structural techniques, created iconic buildings such as the Sagrada Família. His visionary thinking not only revolutionized architecture but also continues to inspire awe and admiration around the globe.

Beyond individual achievements, innovative thinking has driven societal transformations to the extreme. Albert Einstein's theories of relativity revolutionized our understanding of space, time, and energy. Einstein's ability to challenge Newtonian physics and propose revolutionary concepts paved the way for advancements in technology, space exploration, and our fundamental understanding of the universe. The transformative power of innovative thinking is exemplified by Mahatma Gandhi's philosophy of nonviolent resistance. Gandhi's unconventional approach to achieving independence for India through peaceful protest not only challenged the might of the British Empire but also inspired civil rights movements worldwide.

The impact of thinking beyond the obvious extends into shaping the future of humanity itself. Consider the visionary leadership of Marie Curie in the field of radiology and her pioneering research on radioactivity. Curie's ground-breaking discoveries not only earned her Nobel Prizes in Physics and Chemistry but also laid the groundwork for medical treatments and diagnostic techniques that save countless lives today. In a male-dominated world, Curie's perseverance and mind-set set her apart. Similarly, the entrepreneurial spirit of Steve Jobs and his visionary thinking at Apple Inc. revolutionized consumer technology with innovations like the iPhone and iPad. Jobs' ability to anticipate consumer needs, coupled with his uncompromising commitment to design excellence, transformed Apple into one of the most valuable companies in the world. His legacy continues to influence the tech industry and inspire future generations of innovators.

In our current era, marked by complex global issues such as climate change, socio-economic inequality, and geopolitical instability, the ordinary modes of thinking often prove inadequate. They tether us to existing paradigms and conventional approaches that have led to stalemates or incremental progress at best. The pressing need for revolutionary change demands a leap into unconventional thinking. Thinking beyond the ordinary empowers us to envision possibilities that lie beyond the immediate horizon of our understanding. Critical reflection and questioning form the foundation. This involves challenging existing paradigms and assumptions, probing why things are the way they are, and exploring whether alternative perspectives could lead to better outcomes. Transformational thinking embraces interdisciplinary and systems perspectives. It requires understanding the interconnectedness and complexity of issues across various domains – science, technology, economics, sociology, ethics, and beyond. Empathy and human-centredness can help in understanding the lived experiences, needs, and aspirations of individuals, communities, and ecosystems. Courage and risk-taking are inherent to transformational thinking and are essential for overcoming inertia and effecting meaningful change in the face of adversity. Collaboration and collective intelligence are also essential pillars to achieve transformation. Finally, ethical reflection and sustainability are foundational principles. Transformational thinking considers the long-term consequences of actions, promotes fairness and justice, and safeguards the well-being of future generations and the planet.

Changing Perspectives

To be human is to be immersed in the peculiar ballet of eccentricity and intellect. From our earthbound perspectives, we often perceive ourselves as masters of our destiny – innovators and thinkers who shape the course of history. Yet, this perception shifts dramatically when viewed through the eyes of those who venture beyond our atmosphere. Consider the astronomers, explorers of the cosmos, who gaze back upon Earth from the vast expanse of space. From their vantage point, our planet appears as a fragile oasis amidst the cosmic void, a reminder of our smallness in the grand scheme of the universe. This perspective humbles us, prompting introspection about our place and purpose in the cosmos. The contrast between our perceived mastery and the cosmic reality highlights the dual nature of human existence – a simultaneous assertion of agency and a recognition of vulnerability. It reminds us that while we strive to innovate and progress; we are also bound by the limits of our understanding and the constraints of our environment. In this vast and mysterious universe, our actions reverberate far beyond our immediate surroundings, shaping not only our own fate but also the future of life on earth. Thus, to be human is not only to embrace our capacity for creativity and intellectual pursuit, but also to acknowledge our interconnectedness with the cosmos. This shift from earthly mastery to cosmic humility is profound. It urges us to contemplate our origins and interconnectedness with the universe. Our evolution from ancient origins to modern complexities finds context against the backdrop of cosmic insignificance. This broader perspective helps us to embrace humility and acknowledge the fragility of our existence.

Human thought is a formidable force in shaping the world we inhabit. It serves both as a unifying tool and a divisive catalyst, capable of fostering cooperation or sparking conflict depending on how it is wielded. Human thought manifests in myriad forms, from individual beliefs to collective ideologies. This intellectual prowess allows us to collaborate on a global scale, transcend geographical boundaries to achieve shared goals such as scientific progress, cultural exchange, and economic development. Through the exchange of ideas and the pursuit of common objectives, human thought becomes a cornerstone of unity, bridging diverse perspectives and fostering mutual understanding among individuals and nations. However, alongside its potential for unity, human thought also harbours the seeds of dissonance. Differences in beliefs, values, and interpretations often lead to ideological conflicts, social unrest, and even warfare. History bears witness to the power of divergent ideologies to divide societies, pitting individuals and groups against each other in pursuit of conflicting agendas. Leaders across various domains wield significant influence over the direction of human thought and its societal implications.

In politics, leaders formulate policies that shape national and international relations, impacting economies, societies, and environments. Economic leaders make decisions that influence global markets, wealth distribution, and the livelihoods of millions. Meanwhile, ecological leaders guide policies that determine the fate of natural resources and the environment, affecting biodiversity, climate stability, and the sustainability of ecosystems. The decisions made by these leaders reverberate across multiple dimensions of human existence. A policy enacted to promote economic growth may inadvertently exacerbate social inequalities, leading to unrest and protests. Similarly, environmental policies designed to preserve ecosystems may clash with economic interests, sparking debates over resource management and conservation strategies.

The advent of digital communication and information technologies has revolutionized the dissemination of human thought. Social media platforms, online forums, and digital news outlets enable instantaneous sharing of ideas and opinions on a global scale. While this connectivity has the potential to foster dialogue and facilitate collective action, it also amplifies the spread of misinformation, polarization, and extremism. The rapid dissemination of biased or inaccurate information can shape public perceptions, influence decision-making processes, and contribute to societal divisions. Our collective beliefs and attitudes determine the paths we tread as societies and as a global community. When rooted in compassion, justice, and mutual respect, our thoughts foster harmony and sustainable progress. Conversely, when driven by fear, greed, or ignorance, they can lead to strife and devastation. The art of thinking encompasses both the profundity of our origins and the expansiveness of our aspirations. Let us embrace our eccentricities with humility, knowing that in our collective consciousness lies the potential to shape a harmonious existence on this fragile pale blue dot we call home.

***